CU00797051

Beyond Entropy: When Energy Becomes Form

AA Publications

TABLE OF CONTENTS

BRETT STEELE

Entropic Instincts: Architecture as Energy

> 'Many architectural concepts found in science-
> fiction have nothing to do with science or fiction,
> instead they suggest a new kind of monumen-
> tality which has much in common with the aims
> of some of today's artists.'
> *Robert Smithson, Entropy and the New Monuments*

Ours is an era in which both foreign policies and national economies are being shaped by one thing alone: our planet's energy resources. This much we already know, as we do the metanarratives by which we are supposedly gripped in a sudden and torturous spiral of decline and conflict over the undeniable dwindling of these resources. In contrast to such political and commercial concerns, however, it is speculation as to how this reality might be reflected in the production of energy as *culture* that lies at the core of **Beyond Entropy**.

From the increasingly fractured geography of modern petrochemical urbanism to the byzantine infrastructures related to the world's discovery, movement, sale and consumption of water, oil and other natural resources, the context for this publication includes the many and flourishing contemporary forms of speculation regarding our world's near future, as defined by the search for new energy sources. For the past two years, as part of our **Beyond Entropy** research cluster, the students and staff of the AA School have been joined by scientists, artists and others who have come together for the purposes of opening up a multidisciplinary assessment of the distinctly cultural aspects of energy. What lies at the heart of this undertaking – wonderfully curated and directed by the young Italian architect Stefano Rabolli Pansera – is a belief that issues of energy and form are not extraneous to the production of culture, but rather are central to, indeed indistinguishable from, culture itself. And this is where the real leap lies: in the argument of this book, energy is the means by which we might more fully grasp and articulate the very idea of culture today. Such a view is intuitive, reflexive and ultimately incredibly timely and relevant.

In what follows the reader is presented with an index of open speculation on energy in all its complex and conflicting, contemporary manifestations: a matrix, a register of commentary, ideas, discussion and debate provoked during a marathon international symposium arranged by the Architectural Association in summer 2010 and graciously hosted by the Fondazione Giorgio Cini in Venice during the 12th International Biennale of Architecture. Speakers at the symposium were asked to speculate on the role and presence of energy in contemporary human culture, and to do so from the vantage-point of their own forms of professional, academic, theoretical or practical expertise. What followed over the course of more than 11 hours that day was a fascinating, uneven and unexpectedly provocative series of performances during which energy was subject to philosophical, economic, technical and spatial analyses of all kinds – by fiction writers, commodity traders, scientists, engineers, architects, artists, philosophers and others.

On behalf of everyone at the Architectural Association, my thanks go out to everyone involved: to the curator of **Beyond Entropy**, Stefano Rabolli Pansera, for his own considerable, nearly limitless forms of (personal and intellectual) energy; to the participants – speakers and audience – who made the Venice symposium such a highly charged event; to our hosts at the Fondazione Giorgio Cini, who provided an incomparable Renaissance setting on the Grand Canal; to our generous external sponsors and supporters, including Olivetti-

Direct Technology Solutions here in the UK, RePower and Bersi Serlini; to our many media partners including magazines and newspapers in Italy and beyond; and to the many students and staff of the school who made the cluster such a success. The following book offers only a glimpse of all this – a small and partial sampling of the immense insight, intelligence and discovery made possible by the bringing together of so much diverse talent, intelligence, experience and creativity. Even in its partial and fragmentary recording of a remarkable platform that has made Stefano's research cluster so important to our school the past two years, this small publication captures and stores some of **Beyond Entropy's** remarkable amounts of energy – something I'm very pleased we are able to present here to other audiences and participants to re-engage with, reinterpret, and reinvent for their own purposes.

Brett Steele
Director, Architectural Association School of Architecture

Max Planck was thrilled by the fact that work is not dissipated but remains stored for many years, never diminished, latent in a block of stone until, one day, it may happen that this same block falls upon a passerby and kills him. Indeed, in every artist or scientist, the principle of continuation of energy is interlinked with the research of happiness and of death. Even in architecture this research is related to material and to energy; without this observation it is not possible to understand any construction, neither from the static point of view nor from the formal point of view.

Aldo Rossi,
A Scientific Autobiography

At the start of everything is a **decision** – an action that implies the choice of one thing and the refusal of everything else. **Beyond Entropy** started with the recognition that architectural discourse usually considers energy as a technical issue within a larger discourse of sustainability – a model that seems to be offered as the exclusive form of questioning, analysing and articulating the concept of energy. In clear opposition to this **Beyond Entropy** celebrates the concept of energy as a poetic device with which to question and define new relationships between form and space.

We make sense of the reality around us by producing objects and giving form and order to the spaces we inhabit. Through these actions we consume energy and oppose entropy – the ever-growing level of disorder in the universe. Energy, entropy and form are the precepts through which this research operates. Form organises matter and makes it intelligible – it is the source of order, unity and the identity of objects. Entropy is the passage of objects and systems from a state of order to disorder. In terms of energy there seems to be the lack of a critical vocabulary that can describe this notion. Strictly speaking it refers to something that possesses the ability to make nature do work. But what is this something? And what is work? This something is not a force, as energy is defined in contrast to force – in modern physics energy is distinguished from force as the integral is from its function. In a similar way work is defined as the production of physical change through energy. Although it is impossible to define energy without deferring to such tautologies it is possible to describe one essential attribute of energy – that it is always conserved.

There is a fact, or if you wish, a law, governing all natural phenomena that are known to date. There is no known exception to this law – it is exact so far as we know. The law is called the conservation of energy. It states that there is a certain quantity, which we call energy that does not change in manifold changes which nature undergoes. That is a most abstract idea, because it is a mathematical principle; it says that there is a numerical quantity which does not change when something happens. It is not a description of a mechanism, or anything concrete; it is just a strange fact that we can calculate some number and when we finish watching nature go through her tricks and calculate the number again, it is the same.
The Feynman Lectures on Physics

How does the principle of the conservation of energy relate to space? How does energy inform our conventional understanding, control and production of forms? And how can architectural discourse – which is inherently concerned with spatial reasoning, formulating briefs, analysing contexts, representing space and constructing buildings – contribute to a definition of energy? My premise is that space itself is the mode through which energy evolves, in the process transforming all other forces – whether structural, cultural, economic – while ensuring their dispersal and development beyond current forms and parameters. Accordingly the central problem is not that buildings, the city and its adjacent territories consume energy, but rather that space itself manifests the concept of energy. The sustainable position is subverted by the concept of **energy as space**.

Architecture rarely considers this formulation of **energy as space** – this shimmering of time and space that is constantly being transformed and unable to be reduced into form. The primordial energy that allows forms to emerge and dissipate is the destiny of space. How can we reconfigure our architectural tools and categories according to this new energetic paradigm? **Beyond Entropy** subverts the traditional principles through which architects attempt to **govern** space – the notions of Form, Brief, Structure, Context and Representation that have historically been used for the concrete and rational control of space are systematically questioned and reconfigured through the new energetic paradigm. The prototypes, lectures and debates of the **Beyond Entropy** project negate these conventions through a series of unexpected inventions.

Architecture is made possible by the confrontation of a precise form with time and with elements, a confrontation which lasts until the form is destroyed in the process of this combat: the form of a space cannot be detached from its evolution in time... Thus the temporal aspect of architecture no longer resided in its dual nature of light and shadow or, in the aging of things; it rather presented itself as a catastrophic moment in which time takes things back.

Aldo Rossi,
A Scientific Autobiography

ENERGY
AS
FORM

STEFANO RABOLLI PANSERA

Form is not a complete quantifiable entity but the temporary coalescence of a complex system of forces that remain evidentially visible in the form itself. Form emerges, transforms and decays according to the operation of specific temporal forces. In a similar way architectural space is always entangled with time simply because space is itself temporal. Aldo Rossi identified this conception in his relation of form and function. **Form persists and comes to preside over a built work in a world where functions continually become modified,** he wrote, **and in form, material is modified. The material of a bell is transformed into a cannon ball, the form of an amphitheatre into that of a city – the form of a city into a palace.** Time and space cease to be formal containers and become the active producers of form. As forms continuously morph from one state to another, space and time are intertwined and form itself becomes a space–time event.

In this section Antonio Negri highlights how form and energy are incommensurate not just with one another but also with capitalistic forms of accumulation and labour. Matteo Pasquinelli defines the concept of negative entropy as a movement of energy accumulation rather than dissipation. Marco Vanucci focuses on form as a diagram of forces and the relevance of energy in relation to its fabrication. Grazia Francescato argues that the integration of ecological, economic and social forces should inaugurate a new vision and form of life. Angelo Merlino focuses on the form of space immediately after the origin of the universe. Finally, Marco Baravalle describes the decline of urban form and the relevance of entropy as the city's process of becoming territory.

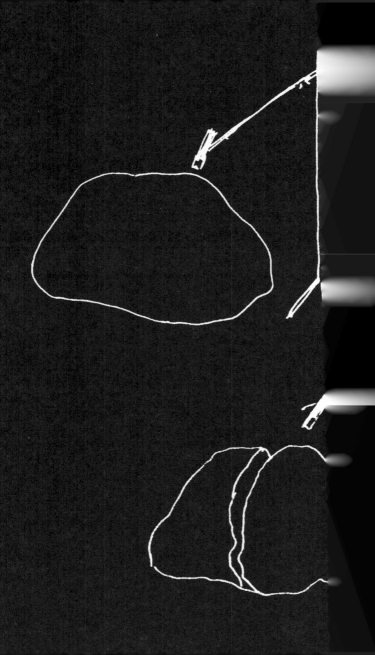

MASSIMO BARTOLINI, SALOTTOBUONO,
DARIO BENEDETTI, RICCARDO ROSSI

Everything has a sound, says Ino Moxo, the shaman from the Amazon. **Tune into the cosmic vibration,** suggests the Hindu Sadhu. Both are anticipating by hundreds of years Max Planck's assertion, at the beginning of the last century, that sound and vibration are among those phenomena which belong to an entropic condition. The difference between these two phenomena is produced during the exercise of energy. There is a slight friction, leading to a transformation of modes, then a moment of rest.

How can a field be defined in which the entropic dérive of the universe can be controlled, produced and made visible by simple human presence? This question is addressed here through a pure field defined by one large circular antenna. The antenna is simultaneously both the perimeter and the centre of the geometry of influence, with sensors that register human alterations and interference in the space. The interferences between the movement of the individual and the imperceptible electric life of an unanimated object are transformed into energy that can be heard even by those who do not enter the field. As in every exchange, it is not obvious that there is a final balance between object, sound and interference. In this way a large amount of effort to produce interference might only produce a small increment of sensibility. Occasionally, however, it happens in the opposite way, with an infinitesimal part of the whole materialising the totality.

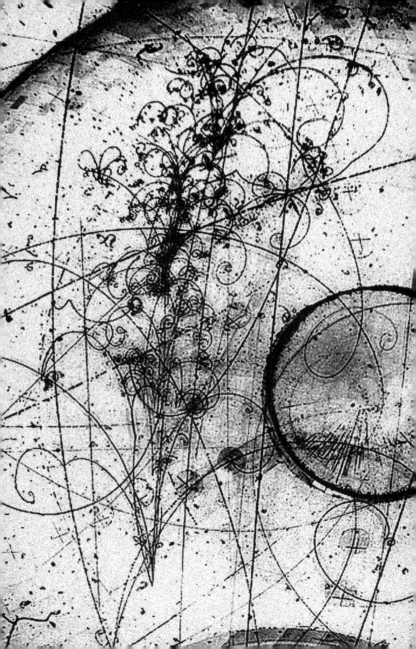

ANGELO MERLINO

Although scientific estimates date the age of the universe at 13.7 billion years, theoretical calculations allow us to understand important phenomena that happened at the point of singularity – so-called Planck Time measured at 10^{-43} seconds. Immediately before Planck Time, the four fundamental forces – gravitation, electromagnetism, strong interaction and weak interaction – were unified and the temperature was immense at 10^{32} K (around 100 million million million million degrees). Gravitation then separated from the other forces and the temperature fell drastically, leading to an event in which the volume of the universe expanded from the size of a tiny proton to the diameter of a small galaxy in a matter of one trillion-trillion-trillionth of a second. In turn the other forces separated and matter and anti-matter emerged. For every one billion particles of anti-matter there were one billion and one particles of matter and when that mutual annihilation was complete this one billionth remained – that's our present universe.

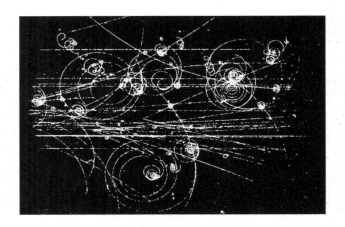

The dystopia o
is naturalised
moralism of 'c

MATTEO PASQUINELLI

Any historical analysis of the uses of **entropy** shows that the initial conception of this notion in physics – which is related to the specific discussion of energy – has been adopted by many other sciences. This can be the source of a dangerous misunderstanding. After an era of techno-determinism I wonder if we are entering an age of energo-determinism – one in which the dystopia of capitalism is naturalised by the moralism of **consuming less**.

apitalism the suming less'.

Any one-dimensional conception of entropy should be contested through the notion of **negative entropy** and by considering those forces that accumulate energy against its dissipation. These are not only natural forces but also those social forces that struggle against the entropy of value governed by capitalism. We should not forget that social autonomy is the first form of resistance against this economic **entropy**.

ANTONIO NEGRI

Activity and work are terms that modern philosophy, ethics and law have taken from political economics and future production planning. In the post-modern era general activities and value-enhancing work tended to be identified with the hegemony of general activity. In the post-industrial/modern era the **de facto subsuming** of society into capital meant that the canonical categories of modern thought and operation – nature and culture, work and technology, factories and society – could no longer be taken for granted.

From a capitalist point of view, the question of **form** is re-opened when the translation of production from value-enhancing work to a dominant general work prevents production from being measured. Capitalism adapted swiftly to this translation by constructing new forms of symmetrical accumulation that match the emergent processes of social and intellectual production. For example, it introduced new enhancement scales and wholly abstract forms of monetary and financial measurement in which industrial value was replaced by the rules and measures of yield – energy yield, real estate and financial yield – that structure the new globalised world. As a result, development is subject to predetermined abstract values, paralysed legislative procedures, unashamedly neo-feudal privilege and incredible – even preposterous – social inequality, and can only assume new forms. Naturally this happens between crises as any kind of value is unaffordable during those moments when timelines are broken and power is epitomised only by violence.

MARCO BARAVALLE

From the 1960s onwards the metropolis began to be read as a field of material and immaterial fluxes. Capitalism structured not only the factory (the means of production) but also society, the city and territories beyond. It was during this period that the idea of **the society as a factory** was born in Italy. The notion of the **città-territorio** – the **city-territory** that expresses the dialectic between reforming tendencies and capitalist governance – became a key concept of urban reform. Architecture was considered as a form of **event** that could break with the constrictions of technocratic or urban planning.

After this initial conceptualisation the idea of the city-territory became progressively marked by an ambivalence that is obvious in 1960s Italian urban planning, especially in the non-stop city – a city without qualities that appears to be based on the archetype of a supermarket, the place in which production and consumption finally overlap. The non-stop city is graphically represented in stark black and white tones, dots, modularity and an endless repetition of sameness. It is simultaneously a device for reproducing the labour force and a space where autonomous forces can accumulate power and – through this accumulation – generate a process of negative entropy.

In recent times the non-stop city seems to have morphed into **junkspace** – the space of material human waste that is a measure of modernity. Junkspace takes an entropic view of global architecture as a burned-out system that can only produce continuous internal spaces consisting of plasterboard, escalators and air-conditioning. As with the city-territory, the networked space of junkspace eliminates any notion of **place** because it negates any notion of the discrete architectural project.

MARCO BARAVALLE

Junkspace ta
view of globa
as a burned-o
can only prod
internal space
of plasterboar
and air-condi

s an entropic
rchitecture
ystem that
e continuous
onsisting
escalators
ning.

GRAZIA FRANCESCATO

I am an avowed heretic. Etymologically, 'heresy' suggests **making a choice**, and the choice we made at the birth of the green movement was rooted in our belief that **you cannot have un-limited growth on a planet with limited resources**. In fact ecosystems and natural resources should lie at the basis of any development because – as Friedrich Engels put it – **resources are but nature transformed**.

We need to integrate the economic and the ecological with one another in order to avoid environmental disruption and the collapse of our current patterns of development. Sustainable choices – and especially energy choices – are not neutral. They should be harbingers of a new vision, a new **weltanschauung** and a new way of life – they should mould a new future. We need the kind of growth that has no limits or boundaries – one that fosters cultural, ethical and spiritual growth. While some might call this naively utopian I agree with the sentiments of Aurelio Peccei, who wrote **the regeneration of human spirit is a real utopia upon which we must lever in order to get out from this situation – it is a fundamental requirement in order to survive and avoid self-destruction**. I think it is time for all of us to be utopians.

IT IS TIME FOR ALL OF US TO BE UTOPIANS

FAR

EQUILIBRIUM

FROM

MARCO VANUCCI

In classical thermodynamics matter always tends towards a state of equilibrium in which energy is released and entropy maximised. However new forms of order – such as self-organisation – arise from phenomena that contradict these classic laws. Self-organisation results from the spontaneous emergence of new structures and new forms of behaviour in unbalanced and open systems.

Thinking about architectural form in terms of the systemic interaction of forces represents a fertile investigative path. This understanding can help us redefine architectural design – shifting from a problem-solving to a problem-caring approach in which the design emerges from the constant interaction of those aspects that inform the project.

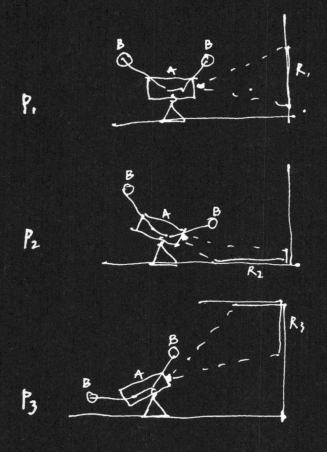

P_1

P_2

P_3

A - SUBJECT

S - SOURCE OF CHAOS

B - ELEMENT THAT RESTORES BALANCE

R - REPRESENTATION OF THE SYSTEM
    (IE: A BODY FALLING)

MASS AND ENERGY

Rubens Azevedo, Ariel Schlesinger, Vid Stojevic

Entropy is the measure of disorder. A built structure has a certain amount of order and a certain amount of entropy. When the building is demolished the order becomes a mess. The material content of the building and its mass are still the same but the matter now takes a different form. The system becomes more entropic. The second law of thermodynamics states that entropy always increases – even though the fundamental laws of nature are symmetrical. A system that is in equilibrium has no flow of information – only by adding interference does the system become active, or entropic.

Imagine a film of a building being imploded. A pair of film projectors are placed on a pendulum projecting an image of the building, which remains motionless as long as the pendulum is motionless. As the pendulum swings in one direction the film is activated and the building collapses. As the pendulum swings back the building comes back together and the system goes on moving back and forth in time. An event which is asymmetrical in time due to the second law of thermodynamics – like the demolition of a building – is rendered symmetrical by the non-chaotic system, in this case the pendulum. The film projector continuously projects this moment of entropy. This is a prototype for a Foucault pendulum that will project a movie whose speed, in both time and space, depends on the rotation of the planet.

Vid Stojevic **If you have a system that works – like a city – and you watch it from above you'll see that it all moves in a regular pattern. And if you were then to introduce something, it would mess up the whole thing. It creates chaos and things operate around it. The chaos is absorbed very quickly. You can find these patterns everywhere. For example, when you take a pendulum and let it swing back and forth it quickly produces a symmetrical movement. If you then introduce a magnet on either side there will be no way to predict the pendulum's movement. After a while, however, it'll settle again into a different pattern.**

Ariel Schlesinger **I notice that something like that happens when I break a tooth. Suddenly I talk differently but after a while I learn to adapt.**

Rubens Azevedo **It's the unconscious part that adapts – as in the case of cities where people will just do something else. If there's a new wall in the beginning it's really annoying but after a while they have to go beyond it so they either climb it or make an opening. Then there are other people – like scientists or architects – who try to solve the problem while others just absorb it. I think these accidents can be quite nice. The printer we'll work with offers the same thing – it's stripped of its own function and needs to be re-contextualised.**

VS **If we get a balancing mechanism to work by using a printer does that mean we're printing something? I wonder what would happen.**

AS **It's really easy to make it work.**

VS **Is it really that easy? It'd be balancing itself and**

printing and – in the beginning – it'll probably have to adjust itself to a kind of equilibrium. It'll probably start by printing garbage before there'll be some sort of pattern to it.

AS We'll connect to the theme of energy through balance and use something from the real world. We'll be cantilevering an object – a mass – and doing something that's against gravity. We'll be lifting something that shouldn't be lifted. We won't only be using a printer for something other than it's normally used for but we'll be putting it in a non-rested position.

VS An essential point is that you need energy to make this thing work because if you turn it off it'll fall over.

AS What I am trying to say is that we should see this essence of an idea as a prototype. So we should make sure the principle is very clear so that our idea has a special impact. At this point I wouldn't even settle on the idea that our prototype will be an object because we could apply this principle to other things.

VS So the principle is extremely general?

AS Conceptually the principle could be very general. You could write a story based on it – for example – in which something happens to a person and that person metaphorically occupies the same position as the printer. They could be completely displaced – in a fragile position – but subject to something that keeps balancing that person.

RA That's very nice! I think we should concentrate on developing this principle. Maybe we could do something with fire?

AS **Another idea is to have a group of different set-ups with the same elements we want to use – the printer, cardboard and fire.**

RA **All these things can also tell the story of a person or a society – it could have a narrative.**

AS **I like this idea of the story. It doesn't need to be told in a specific way, but it should allow you to put together an image of somebody.**

VS **We could even have a film about a man.**

RA **We don't necessarily need to put a man into the narrative. Maybe the viewer adds up all of these elements and makes it into a narrative about the man.**

AS **You could also invert that. You can take what is going on in the set-ups we come up with, make those set-ups, register them and then construct a story on top of them – the outcome would be a typical narrative. Then you'll have it both ways. You can let the printer take the role of the man in this mechanical play or you can have the man that is the printer.**

RA **Imagine a space where the viewers can interact with two objects that are in a state of fragility in which they're either balancing themselves or putting the viewers in dangerous situations. You will only have the machines so the viewers will construct the narrative. It would be good to do more research on a specific incident or person. Would it be possible, for example, to remove all of the narrative in this room in such a way that the whole thing can still function as a narrative?**

AS **Of course. In some sense that's what happens with an exhibition – the audience moves through the space and either gets the situation or sees it in a completely different way. I think it's a fun way to develop an idea. In general I feel that this is what I'm missing in my own work because I always think from the end. I think it'll be very interesting to find out how these feelings can be translated into reality or found in the real world.**

VS **I think we can combine all of this. I don't have any problem with only having machines in the room but I wonder if we can make them more than just objects?**

RA **I think we can do that by not making up a story but rather by finding a situation that is experiential or something a specific scientist happened on in their work. We could even look at the journey he took to discover it, or it could be a house, which would be an entirely different situation. But I don't think it should be the objects first and then the narrative. It should be the opposite. We've already decided we'll work with the printer. Now we can put it aside and go back to the other things we have.**

VS **We have the printer, the car, the motorbike and the candles.**

AS **Do you know the work of Peter Fischli and David Weiss?**

RA **Yes of course – the video 'The Way Things Go'. But they also have this work called 'Equilibres' with all these balancing objects. They basically took a bunch of objects and tried to take them as far as they possibly could through their moments of balance. It's a series of photos – they're really remarkable.**

VS I like the idea of burning film because it burns so quickly and contains so much information.

RA If you take a projector and control the film that runs through it then it should be able to balance itself. If the projection is standing on something balanced then the image will go back and forth and also be tilted up and down!

AS Maybe the image could connect to that movement – it could be the projection of a massive cantilevering rock.

RA I think the projected movement will need to run faster than a cantilevering rock because while these machines are running and trying to balance themselves the image will be going back and forth quite fast. Somehow we'll need to shift the weight between one wheel and another. When the film is running it'll move at a different speed.

AS Perhaps we can slow down the speed of the balancing movement. It's important that as it's balancing it's controlling something else – as with the music or printed-paper ideas. The principle was correct but it was too random somehow. It'll be more interesting if the printer, the car or the candles are controlling something else because then it's not just an object – it'll be an object that's doing something else.

RA So the movie will come first. Then the printer.

AS Yes. So what controls the balance?

VS A physical principle should control it. It's just an idea but you could have something burning uncontrollably and something else that controls that burning. When the candle is burning, for example, the lighter or mechanical thing could control this burning and balance the second thing.

RA That's very interesting – something that's uncontrolled and something that's controlled. Or something that's controlled and something that's uncontrolled that keeps it in balance.

AS Then we're missing the idea of stripping the object of its original function because the projector will also function as a projector.

RA I think that's okay.

AS Yes. But what if we have this central controlling thing that isn't balancing itself but is controlling the balance of something else.

RA I don't like that so much because I think this is exactly the power of our objects – they're all self-contained. Sometimes when you try to be overly complicated you lose the legibility. It's nice when someone approaches something and it's all there in front of their eyes.

VS If you have this object moving backwards and forwards it'll be very beautiful. You could also have something moving ridiculously slowly so you'd need to spend a lot of time in the space to appreciate it.

AS I'm still missing something but I think we agree on the principle – that we're modifying the function of every-thing. We'll use it to maintain something outside of each object's rested position.

VS Have you thought about the practical side? You'll

need to do some reverse engineering.

RA You'll need a gyroscope.

AS What we'll build will probably be a completely new projector – it'll be a machine.

RA It'll be completely new but it will look old.

AS I think the movement should be a little slower so you can read what we put on the screen better.

VS You could either have a slow and natural process or different things moving at different speeds. I don't have a concrete idea but it could be like a growing plant that will adapt itself to its natural environment. That could take three weeks and be a good example of an extremely slow process!

RA It could also be a slide projector with a cartridge of slides. The more the slides are stacked towards the end of the cartridge the more it tilts in a certain direction. But to go back – the machine has to go back with all the slides.

VS The cool thing about that is that it's precisely about entropy. It fits perfectly. You have something that doesn't make any sense when it goes backwards – it's like the video I showed where you see a bullet going through a tomato and when you rewind the video you see the bullet coming out.

RA Could you explain what entropy is?

VS Entropy is the measure of disorder. If you have a tomato and a bullet, for example, you have an order system that has a certain amount of order or a certain amount of entropy. Then when the bullet destroys the tomato the order becomes a mess but you still have the bullet and the mess of tomato, which is increased entropy. The second law of thermodynamics says that entropy always increases – even though the laws of nature are symmetrical – and it's extremely unlikely that while you'll see the tomato exploding you'll never see it spontaneously coming back together again.

AS We can apply this idea in a very simple way, for example as a concrete slab that's cracking. The projector will somehow suspend the slab in the air and when the film finishes it'll crack. That was the idea and holding the block in the air until it cracks is very poetic.

RA But the film won't finish because the machine keeps balancing backwards and forwards.

AS I would like the object to crack. The film we see on the projection should show a similar thing – something that moves back and forth, has weight and mass and is cracking. The conceptual beauty is that the thin and fragile film actually holds all of this.

RA Great. So the film could also be about someone who's about to murder someone else but as he approaches the victim and is about to stab him, the projector will bounce back and the murder will never happen – so the work will always remain trapped in that moment. Visually it could also be very arresting.

VS The construction of the projector will probably introduce lots of good ideas on how to approach this.

RA We could install the printer mechanism inside the

projector. Then the same mechanism that controls the mechanism of the weight also controls the mechanism of the backwards and forwards movement. So we will be cheating a bit because it won't be the actual object that's controlling the weight but it will move in a synchronised manner so the viewer will understand it as the same thing. Personally I always believe in doing it the 'real' way, but the visual aspect will be the film going forwards and then going backwards. It needs to move slowly so that the viewer can perceive this movement.

VS So do you let it do its own thing? Move randomly backwards and forwards?

RA Yes. I don't think we should program it. Sometimes the guy will be shot and sometimes he won't.

VS I like that better.

RA I think we should invent an autonomous system – one that we can't control at all. I also don't think it should only go backwards and forwards – it should be more random.

AS What if we go back to the idea of the room and instead of projecting on a screen we project it anywhere in the room, then the movement can do many other things.

RA No, no! Why?

AS Relax. It's just an idea. We can complicate everything now and then take it out later. Don't worry! I'm just trying to find a way of making what you're suggesting work because if it's just like you suggest

– moving backwards and forwards by a hidden mechanism – then it will be controlled.

VS I guess that if we're cheating then you can cheat far
enough to make it behave in an interesting and random
way.

RA No. We shouldn't – that's why I don't like cheating.

VS I have the feeling we'll have to because if you don't
it'll settle into something that fits and isn't repetitive.
If you let the machine do its own thing it'll eventually
end up making the same movements in a regular pattern.

RA When we looked at the printer its movements
looked really random.

VS You'll have to introduce some source of chaos, which
could exist in the printer because it's so finely balanced.
It'll be more difficult to introduce chaos into slower
moving things.

RA And what about the slide projector?

AS The slide projector won't work at all. It's a nice idea
and has the same principle but if it's already complicated
with the printer, a slide projector will jam the machine
even more. You can't have a slide projector going back
and forth to such a degree.

VS I think the nicest thing is the film going back and
forth.

AS I don't think we should worry about the technical restrictions at this point. We have a good principle
now – it's a machine that balances itself through its own

mechanism that continuously projects this 'entropy-moment'.

VS **It's breaking the second law of thermodynamics.**

AS **It's breaking the second law of thermodynamics? With that kind of quote it's perfect! It's a good idea, it's a principle and it's a mechanism – now we'll just have to figure out how it'll work. I do think though that we should work toward pushing the two elements – entropy and mass – a little bit more.**

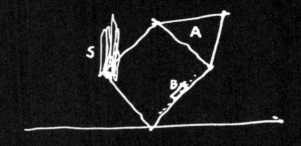

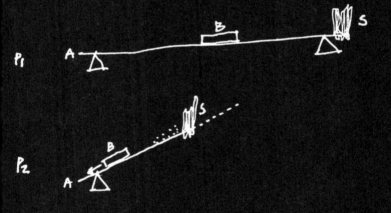

A - SUBJECT
S - SOURCE OF CHAOS
B - ELEMENT THAT RESTORES BALANCE

*Similarly, architecture becomes
the vehicle for an event we desire,
whether or not it actually occurs;
and in our desiring it, the event
becomes something progressive
in the Hegelian sense. It is for this
reason that the dimensions of a
table or a house are very important,
not, as the functionalist thought,
because they carry out a determined
function, but because they permit
other functions. Finally because they
permit everything that is unfore-
seeable in life.*

Aldo Rossi,
A Scientific Autobiography

ENERGY
AS
BRIEF

STEFANO RABOLLI PANSERA

Energy subverts a fixed notion of brief in favour of the free interplay of virtual uses and dimensions. Instead of defining the functionality of form, the energetic brief is concerned with the possibilities of form and spatial inhabitation. The continuous transformation of form suggests a spatial production that does not produce objects but rather relationships to context – with the emergence of new relationships between objects giving rise to new meanings and programmes.

The potential energy prototypes dissolve the concept of the discrete work through a series of proposals that question the possibilities of what an artwork could be. Judith Revel focuses on the ontological value of artistic creation and defines its force as a coherent deformation of forces that are rooted in subjective experience. Bonnie Camplin investigates the relationship between invention, intention and sensation by considering the artwork as a mode for generating anarchy. Jos de Gruyter and Harald Thys demonstrate the existence of parallel worlds and the possibility of inhabiting those worlds through a mental displacement. Alessio Satta observes how the memory of past mining activities in the Sardinian town of Buggerru suggests a new programme for developing the town. Finally, Joseph Rykwert and Javier Castañon both focus on the possibility of reversing the cycle of consumption by suggesting how the disposal of waste is an opportunity for a new architectural brief.

MY INTENTION IS PERFECT ANARCHY

I propose an understanding of instinctive artistic practice as a generator of anti-entropic wealth and an anarchic release.

JUDITH REVEL

I believe we should unite – in the name of the creative power – the singular and material history of 'local' spatial determinations and the inaugural world with its creative twists and deformations. In his writings from the 1950s Maurice Merleau-Ponty assigned an ontological status to artistic creation and defined its power as a coherent deformation rooted in subjective experience. Such an experience does not require a stable subjectivity but proceeds through a series of **imbalances** – movements, openings of lines, and the emptying and re-filling of reality – until it is no longer possible to distinguish between the transformation and the invention.

Artistic creation is a sort of Janus figure for Merleau-Ponty, one that is never external to the determinations and material process of history but is able to create a **coherent deformation** of the words, syntax, colours and shapes which lie within this mesh of history. It is this deeply creative action that produces subjectivity in the world and – as Maurice Merleau-Ponty stated – **there is no definitive system because the revolution is the regime of creative imbalance**. In these terms the production of subjectivity, the networking of singularities and the deformative and political opening of worlds are all against entropy.

There is no definitive system because the revolution

is
the regime
of
creative
imbalance.

Maurice Merleau-Ponty

JAVIER CASTAÑON

If entropy measures the level of disorder in a given system, then entropy should be one of the first measures in design – like checking the fuel levels before starting a journey. In time our design decisions can be measured by how well or how efficiently we are using energy.

For example, for years the design of car headlamps was taken for granted. The sheet steel would be manufactured with a hole in it, which needed to have a rebated edge onto which the six pieces – reflector, lens, trim, etc. – making up the head-lamp would then be screw-fixed, using a total of 12 or more screws. So in order to replace the lamp seven distinct steps were necessary. In order to make a hole in sheet steel you use a great deal of energy. To rebate the edge of a hole in sheet steel you have to use even more energy. This was the way cars were made. In 1972 the public saw a big change. The lamp and headlamp became a single component but the interesting de-velopment was that the headlamp became the meeting point of three panels, in which we did not have to make a hole and which were not welded or riveted but independently fixed to the chassis and simply met around the headlamp. Ever since then headlamps have been designed without having to make holes in sheet steel that was the most costly, in energy terms, of all the processes mentioned above.

Although we can talk about creativity we are not really creating but rather transforming. Our ability to transform forms depends on our ability to ride the energy path as it is transformed in each and every change.

This project considers how entropy varied during the evolution of Buggerru, a small mining village in southwest Sardinia. The memory of the village resides in the ruin of the hospital that opened with the first mine in 1875. All of the villagers were familiar with this building – the current generation was born there – and the village had grown around it. The hospital was closed at the same time as the mines and in 2010 the Conservatoria delle Coste agency transformed the derelict hospital into a zero-emission hostel, creating a new development model for Buggerru that was not only based on the building's architectural qualities but also its inviting human qualities.

JOS DE GRUYTER, HARALD THYS

parallelle wereld

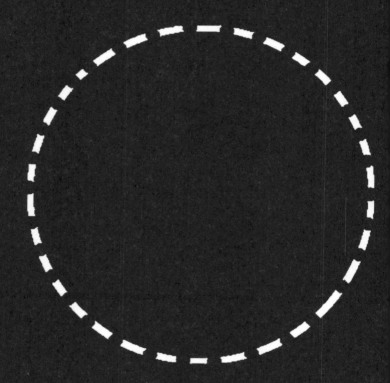

Parallel Worlds

echte wereld

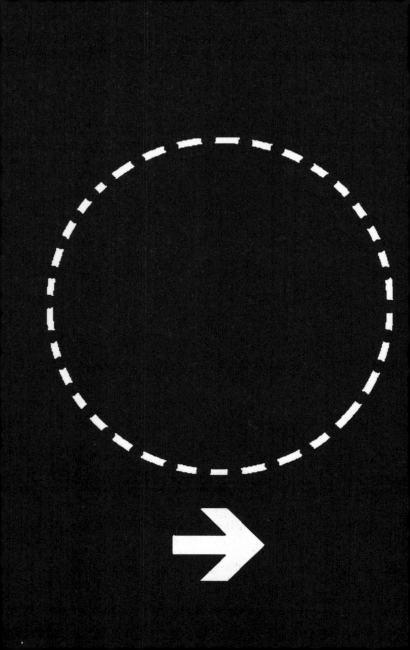

JOSEPH RYKWERT

While the relation between the city as imaged consumer and its consolidated worldwide hinterland can be effectively organised, it is much more difficult to manage the evacuation and disposal of all the detritus that is the correlate of consumption.

And while consumption was taken over by industry and business, evacuation, excretion and waste have become increasingly bulky and its management taken over by organised crime rather than legitimate trade. But then we are dealing with subterranean matters.

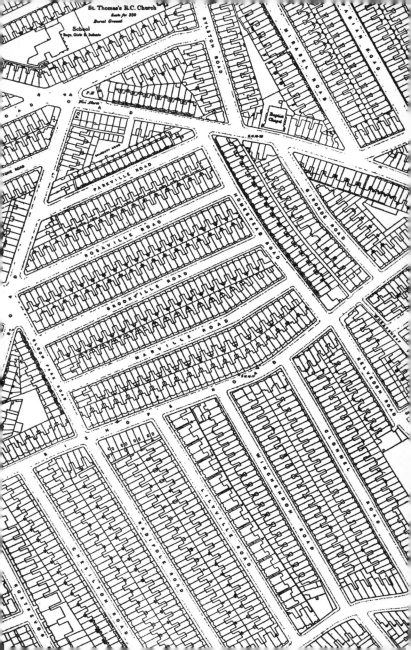

St. Thomas's R.C. Church
Seats for 850
Burial Ground

School
Boys, Girls & Infants

P.H.

PARKVILLE ROAD

ROSAVILLE ROAD

BROOKVILLE ROAD

MARVILLE ROAD

POTENTIAL ENERGY
Peter Liversidge, Julian Loeffler, Roberto Trotta

It is fascinating to contemplate how a rock can stay still in precarious equilibrium on a cliff for thousands of years, only to fall abruptly, its potential energy – silently stored for so long – finally released. Yet the moment potential energy is released is also the moment of its expenditure, as the infinite number of potential outcomes is reduced to a single burst of real energy. Potential energy cannot be directly observed, therefore, and we can only imagine its existence through theoretical constructions or mathematical calculations. Spaces are designed to allow the potential for certain events to take place within them by defining spatial limitations, creating order and resisting entropy. There is a fine line between potential and its realisation, however, and neither a chessboard nor a football pitch will tell you who is going to win the game.

The prototype is a distant relative of the pinball machines, table football games, tennis courts, swimming pools and football pitches that are present in every city around the world. Like these examples the prototype is a stand-alone entity that explores the balance between the rigidity of its spatial organisation and the unpredictability of the events within. Visitors are invited to invest energy on one side while the other side is slowly charged like a spatial battery. Once the system has been saturated it remains – like the rock on the cliff – precariously balanced.

Peter Liversidge **It would be good to start off by discussing what the idea of 'potential' means to each of us. When I found out we would be working in a group the exciting thing for me was the possibility of the unknown – the potential for things to go right or wrong. Mistakes are very important for me. When I'm writing or typing on a keyboard I don't really mind if I hit the wrong key. It's fascinating to me that you put faith in people to experience your work in ways that are out of your control. It's this possibility that I am interested in as much as the outcome. To be honest, I probably didn't think about the notion of potential before being asked to think about it, neither did I really think about the potential of the projects before. But it's quite a good way to look at it. You realise that sometimes the first mark you make is either incredibly right or incredibly wrong. Sometimes you just need to get a new piece of paper or you just work around that mistake – it's a starting point.**

Julian Loeffler **Often mistakes are all you need to start creating something and take a step forward. I relate this to the idea of experimentation because I think it's interesting how one can create those extremely specific but unlikely conditions in the creative process. This is where accidents happen, which lead you to completely different outcomes to what you had planned. If you look at science or art, many discoveries have been made by mistake, with somebody who's determined to get one result ending up with something else entirely.**

Roberto Trotta **There are also those inventions that create conditions which are almost unnatural.**

PL **That's exactly what I was thinking about the CERN**

experiments. How do they know what the Big Bang actually was? How do they know what they are re-creating by forcing these tiny microscopic objects or atoms through those two little tubes?

RT It's tied in with the notion of potentiality in the laws of nature. Whatever happens when those particles are smashed together has to occur in accordance with the laws of nature, which over time have become highly manmade – it seems to me – because we recreate the conditions in which these potential laws can express themselves. The existence of strange physical systems such as two-dimensional electron gases is an example that has always struck me. Essentially these gases are confined to two dimensions and have only been created over the last ten years or so through various experiments. Although it's quite plausible that two-dimensional electron gases have never existed naturally, the laws of nature allow for two-dimensional gases – their special properties were always out there. So in a way its potential lies in beating nature at its own game through the creation of new conditions. The potential for such conditions was always there, but nature itself didn't quite realise it could be done.

JL If the potential is infinite, is everything potentially possible?

RT Well general physics would say that everything that is not explicitly forbidden is possible. So yes, every-thing is possible.

JL So then what is forbidden?

RT Well, things like violating the principle of the con-servation of energy is forbidden.

JL It's like the constant speed of light. It's something you work your theory around. And it depends on what you are willing to bend and how you are willing to bend it. In some ways it's quite a nice analogy for what we're doing, which has all the potential to get it wrong and an equal potential for it to work or to do exactly what's been imagined. You need the effort of pushing something to the limit.

PL And to accept that it's not necessarily going to work and if it doesn't that's all right. The acceptance of failure is so important because the potential for failure is always there. If you can get away from the fear of failure then you can do much more.

JL Failure is actually a very strange term – in some ways it can be quite heroic. It's not really a failure if something unexpectedly spectacular happens, but what if almost nothing happens?

PL That's exactly what science needs. When you know that everything you've assumed is wrong then you're in the perfect place for science.

RT You're right that scientific failure can be positive. The worst case scenario is...

JL To know everything!

RT Where it doesn't even fail so there's nothing wrong!

JL Exactly. Because if it fails properly then it didn't actually fail at all. If things fail but you're able to see what you didn't expect then that's good. But if the machine doesn't work properly then that's a costly failure.

JL What about the role of the limits you place in the process?

PL That's quite interesting. I've never really spoken about the way I work. I don't want to sound arrogant but I know things won't fail because I've done it before. For example, if I'm in the studio and I think something might not work I'll never show it.

JL I don't really know how different it is between the scientific or artistic endeavour because if you're thrown off path you often end up doing something else which works better for you and you end up doing it better. Maybe that's more difficult to do in a scientific context where the rules are clearly set and you can't deviate so easily. I don't think you can just go with the path of least resistance – at some point you have to change direction. This is probably similar in research.

PL I think it is. We are all basically discovering things.

JL I was also thinking about these differences and similarities. It's really quite striking how this relates to the topic of entropy. What's different is how we deal with it. In my understanding, the scientist tries to understand and explain his own sculpture around these concepts, which in turn becomes the basis for constructing a theory. In architectural terms there's always some form of construction involved – not necessarily as bricks and mortar but always in terms of construction that speaks of the reduction of entropy or the introduction of some sort of order that goes against nature and the natural course toward entropy. The artist then comes and subverts it again – there are fundamentally different approaches towards this topic.

RT I was struck by something you said in that the whole of life – biologically, culturally, intellectually and perhaps even existentially – is a struggle against entropy.

JL Life itself is an anti-entropic force that is constantly progressing toward death. Like us.

PL Well we all have this tendency to die. There isn't anything we can do about it – you know that at some point your body will fail.

JL You see that's the thing – you can't ignore this topic. Whether you're an architect, artist or scientist you have to take a position toward it. If I build a wall, I have to make a decision and I have to take a position. And that's how you take positions – you don't have a choice.

PL It's your responsibility. But you have that by being an architect, a scientist or an artist.

JL But is this really valid for scientists? Can you see it like this?

RT There is this idealised image of scientists as people who don't take a position because we are objective, impartial or neutral.

PL But if you think about how science is presented it always purports science is fact so it's fascinating that science isn't fact and there's no certainty in it. People look for certainty.

RT Scientists know that is not the case. Only non-scientists think like that.

JL That's precisely what we're saying – science is not about fact and truth, it's about controlling the degree of uncertainty. A few weeks ago I started a book by writing 'You may not realise it but our lives are ruled by uncertainty'. The most difficult part of any book is the first sentence and I presume for scientists it's exactly the same – uncertainty is everything. Was there one specific point in your life on which everything turned?

RT I can definitely say no.

PL I can actually definitely say yes. I remember when I was quite young and I watched a programme on an artist called J.S. Boggs who forged money by drawing banknotes. What I really remember is that while he was staying in a hotel in New York for two or three months, he did these beautifully intricate drawings of American dollar banknotes. When he came to pay for the hotel – and we're talking a massive bill here – he presented three of these drawings. What really struck me was that he was able to pay for his accommodation like this.

JL It's important to talk about how we approach our different subject areas and pose different questions. For example, the kind of research I pursue might pose questions that sound quite scientific but they aren't scientific. Sometimes the concepts come from the field of science. For example, you spoke about 'rarefaction' and the film I made is called 'The Search for Rarefaction'. It's a laboratory term that I borrowed because I wanted to explore it in terms of experiential space. Rarefaction was an idea that could be used to estimate the consciousness of our environmental experience, which can't be sufficiently described in a scientific space–time concept.

RT **Is the space you're talking about more than XYZ coordinates? Is it more a conception of space?**

JL **Yes. Although it's very difficult not to talk about this in a scientific way because talking about rarefaction means talking about light. But then you also have memory – when looking at cinema what you call the 'moving image' is made up of two separate images – one that is frozen like an immobile section plus the addition of a uniform abstract time. The created movement is different from the real movement, yet they're inseparable. When you have a system in which something is changed it results in a translation of movement within that system. As architects we design and work in three-dimensional spaces but there is also an element of abstract space which doesn't exist in three-dimensions. That's why we started to work with video because we wanted to format time and explore qualitative change.**

PL **You used video to describe space and how when you break down those elements within an image you discover those memories that have been frozen within the image – something that represents those split seconds of constant change we touched on earlier.**

JL **As I get older I notice how my memories are complete invention to the point where I think I've done something I actually haven't done.**

RT **Going beyond reality in terms of both history and memory is essential. Science tends to appropriate whatever it looks at even by objectifying those experiences that are intensely human and fictional.**

PL **This is the idea that the fiction provides a unique potential. If we take this idea to a logical conclusion we** don't need to do anything but wait for the potential to be realised.

JL But how can we make a project?

PL It's funny because from this conversation I've thought of making some works already! I thought about coin tossing – where we toss coins onto a certain space – and the notion of probability. Our two-and-a-half hour conversation has led us to the same conclusion. Is that conclusion actually important?

JL Or is it actually a conclusion?

PL I appreciate we've been asked to produce something. We can go about it by brainstorming, or organically or we can start with a model – you could come up with a structure, I could come up with the text.

JL I think we should try to narrow down our brief so we can focus and bring depth to the work at all levels.

PL We could work on the proposals together. You could make something based on text where the outcome takes in everything whether it is a negotiation of space or not. Our prototype could be the spoken word or anything else.

JL That's a big question. What would this prototype be?

RT It might be something you can imagine, some kind of installation prototype.

JL I think it would be better to see this prototype as a chronological structure – we keep what we did in the first instance and then develop it on from there.

PL **That could be good. I think what you're writing now on that piece of paper could be our prototype – shown on a plinth as a single piece of paper with the fingerprints and marks where you had lunch. Using it as a prototype is just the freeing up of a form. Maybe whenever we get together we can write down the things we discuss and that becomes our prototype. It will allow us to get away from the idea of the prototype being an object.**

RT **I like the subversion of having the working draft as the prototype. But I'd also like this to engage the audience or public in a more immediate way and be something they can respond to in a way that doesn't require them to know the history behind it.**

PL **I agree. But that's the idea behind a prototype as something that is 'proto' and isn't going to be anything other than the first step of a further development. Perhaps our project stops at the prototype.**

*In San Carlone at Arona the limits
that distinguish the domain of
architecture, the machine and
instruments were dissolved in
marvellous inventions. As with the
Homeric horse the pilgrim enters
the body of the saint as he would
a tower or a wagon. After he mounts
the exterior stair of the pedestal,
the steep ascent through the interior
of the body reveals the structure
of the work and the welded seams of
the huge pieces of metal sheets.
Finally he arrives at the interior-
exterior of the head, from the eyes
of the saint, the view of the lake
acquires infinite contours, as if
one were gazing from a celestial
observatory.*

Aldo Rossi,
A Scientific Autobiography

ENERGY
AS
STRUCTURE

STEFANO RABOLLI PANSERA

The notion of structure is fundamental to recognising and understanding form and the physical organisation that supports it. Alberti's notion of **firmitas** specifically refers to a structural rigidity that – by opposing gravity – keeps a form **in place**. In architectural terms the tectonics of a building corresponds to the form of the space within it and its structural support. Energy adds the notions of time and ambiguity to this concept of structure to become a machine for the transformation of form. The energetic structure does not preserve form but rather dissolves it to facilitate a continuous becoming that changes temporally to reveal the distortion of space. Any hierarchy between supporting and supported elements is dissipated and the ambiguity between these components subverts the perception and the recognition of form itself.

The mechanical prototype revises Alfred Jarry's time-machine and utilises momentum to reveal the similarity of space and time. Tania Saxl explores how the laws of mechanics are affected by scale through a consideration of the mechanics of a microscopic bacterium. Finally the programme of Nikolaus Hirsch's Cybermohalla Hub shifts between production and display – with structural and non-structural elements becoming indistinguishable from one another.

As you get down to the size
of a bacterium the physics
of its environment is completely
different to what we experience
in our macroscopic world.
Because of its minute size the
movement of a bacterium
can be likened to swimming
through tar or concrete. If the
motor stops rotating there
won't be any inertia – it won't
keep spinning but will stop
dead within 1/10 of an Angstrom.
This motor is truly an astounding
feat of engineering.

The Cybermohalla Hub is never finished. It's an institutional experiment in flux that can grow from one to two to three to four storeys. Space becomes so precarious that separated elements are blended into one and elements like cupboards, shelves, display boards and work desks become load-bearing structures.

The institution grows with its production of texts, documents, videos and objects and in a mode that oscillates between production and display.

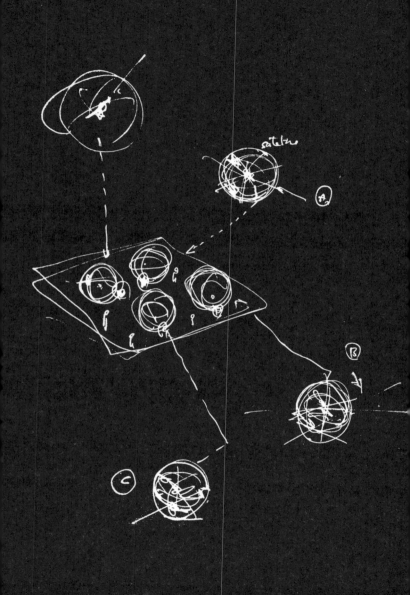

satelit

A

B

C

MECHANICAL ENERGY
Shin Egashira, Andrew Jaffe, Attila Csorgo

During the late nineteenth century many artists and scientists began to look at space and time differently. Guided by the discovery of non-Euclidean geometry they explored questions of space and time in the years before Einstein formulated his revolutionary mathematical theories of special and general relativity. The French writer Alfred Jarry, for example, created a pseudo-science called 'pataphysics' that led him to theorise a time-machine which would be 'A Machine to isolate us from Duration, or from the action of Duration (from growing older or younger, the physical drag which a succession of motions exerts on an inert body) will have to make us "transparent" to these physical phenomena, allow them to pass through us without modifying or displacing us. This isolation will be sufficient if Time, in overtaking us, gives us a minimal impulse just great enough to compensate for the deceleration of our habitual Duration conserved by inertia.'

In order to realise this machine, Jarry employed such nineteenth-century physical concepts as angular momentum, the polarisation of light and, most importantly, 'luminiferous aether', which Einstein's work eventu-ally showed to be non-existent. At the core of Jarry's machine was a cube of giant mechanical flywheels crafted from ebony and copper, quartz and ivory. Our twenty-first century prototype updates his machine by using electric motors, computer-cut plywood, ball-bearings, bicycle parts and digital cameras. Following Jarry's notion of pataphysics, these components work together to spin at such speed as to resist all forces, eventually resisting our motion through not just space but time itself.

Andrew Jaffe **My initial reaction to the stuff you've already done is that it would probably be easiest to tweak it to things that I know about but maybe that's boring to you?**

Attila Csorgo **No. Go ahead – I'll listen to you!**

AJ **So these are some of your solids. And the reason this interests me is that it's possible the universe is made up of these things, repeated endlessly. So it's a typology. I'll give you an analogy – do you remember the game 'Asteroids'? There are these asteroids and you are this little guy and you're trying to shoot them. Note what happens when you shoot here [points on screen] – the beam pretends to be attached. If you think about what that means, this wrapping around from there to there, to make a cylinder, and then from top to bottom so it's a torus. This is two-dimensional but in higher dimensions you can do the same thing with a cube, tetrahedron, or hexagon, although it's complicated. Basically there's only a finite number of ways you can do it because you have to be able to tile – just imagine a surface where you have to be able to repeatedly place the same shape with no gaps.**

AC **Like Islamic patterns.**

AJ **Exactly. It has to be repetitive in order to make sense. So far I've talked about tiling, or making typology on a flat surface, but in cosmology the universe can be curved like the surface of a sphere. How many ways can you tile the surface of a sphere? The answer is a very small number – it's much harder than tiling. Another way of doing this is to make narrower and narrower slices in the same shape – like orange slices – but in the terms of the universe that's not applicable because the** universe is longer in one dimension and shorter in the other, so that's not a good possibility. I think you can imagine lots of interesting ways to realise this when the universe is shaped less like a sphere and more like a saddle. It's hyperbolic in three dimensions and tiling a hyperbolic surface is even more complicated than tiling a sphere. It's a really difficult mathematical problem.

Shin Egashira **What is regularity in the hyperbolic?**

AJ **This is one [shows example]. You can fit it into a hyperbola but it's much more complicated to figure out mathematically – it has only been possible in the last 20 years or so. What this has to do with my science is that – if we go back to the beams in 'Asteroids' – you can see repeated patterns. But imagine now that the universe has these weird connections and you take a screen that is actually a sphere, which means each point is the same. That's what makes it so complicated, because these points are never the whole picture – they are just little points that match.**

SE **But in reality the idea of a sphere is notional in terms of the universe.**

AJ **Yes it's notional. But right now there's a sphere that is one light minute away from me – which is all the light that could have gotten to me from a minute ago to now. It's notional in the sense that there's no Plexiglas sphere somewhere but it still makes perfect sense. And this is exactly what a sphere is – it's from a particular time and traces this particular time. I described it last night as the surface of a cloud – there is no real surface to a cloud – nonetheless it's a very good approximation to think of it as a surface that is very similar to this.**

AC It would be very beautiful if clouds were spherical in shape!

SE Maybe to start off we could start thinking of topics as the motivation behind the work. What would you call your overall agenda for example? Normally artists have a much clearer idea of this than architects – you can say the work is about this or that.

AC I don't know – I always feel there's an obsessive drive that you can't explain.

SE Maybe we can try to react to yesterday's conversation?

AC I see a lot of similarities with your practice. The mapping of space is very interesting for me but I usually try to show an image of the space – a photo or a representation – that is different to the norm. It's not a simple photo but something completely different and this is how I'd explain my 'drive' in a simplified way.

SE There are two aspects here – your platonic forms and then these transformations. One is about structure and those complexities and transformations that can be described geometrically. On the other hand it shows the impossibility of describing a perfect geometry. I think that the architect's or artist's spatial view definitely borrows certain things from science in order to apply them to a particular agenda. But why has geometry become your subject?

AJ Why? [Laughs]

SE Yes. You're using it to exemplify something complex. Is there an aesthetic to it? Or are you mainly interested in mathematical equations?

AC I know what I'm making with mathematical shapes and solids is not a mathematical revolution but it does reference the world of mathematics because the shapes, tetrahedrons or squares are very 'burdened', be it philosophically or culturally. I like it that all of these elements are in the piece. I originally studied painting but after a certain point painting was too shapeless. I didn't know when a picture was good or bad so I tried to find better frames – I dealt with it in a physical and mathematical way.

AJ We could say that we all use cameras. In a way all these cameras also look at one thing at a time – we literally look at one part of the sky. So it's making a timeline of all these different parts and then rolling it back into a map of the sky.

AC Is there some sort of diagram to explain this relationship between the cameras, monitors and scanners?

AJ There are lots of diagrams. What we do is we wait until we see a very bright thing – like Jupiter for example – then we reconstruct what we've been told through existing diagrams. When Jupiter is somewhere other than these diagrams tell us, we know these diagrams aren't right. We can then figure out exactly how the diagram works and explain how these diagrams and models can be fixed.

SE Isn't all of this light from the distant past?

AJ Yes. These lights are 15 billion years old. Light moves in all possible directions but we only see the rays coming toward us. That's why it's not always trivial to figure this all out. So here is our galaxy and the Milky Way – and a lot of other stuff we don't really care about – and we have to learn how to clean these maps. This cleaning is very difficult and forms one of the big challenges. Most of these photons – or light particles – are 15 billion years old but some of them are only a few thousand years old. And some are only a microsecond old when we see them. As an example we have a picture from the Kobe satellite that was launched in 1989. This satellite had blurry spectacles and could only see about seven degrees so it blurred out everything inside seven degrees. Another project I worked on 12 years ago was 10 degrees by 10 degrees – so they all have different resolutions and we can only see a tiny part of the sky at a time.

AC So these are all taken from different points to make one spherical 360° perspective?

AJ Yes, it's all taken from space and so the coordinate system has nothing to do with the earth.

SE So where are we on this map?

AJ We are in the centre – but that's not really a meaningful answer because it's really all around us. You have complete freedom to change the coordinate system.

SE So your camera has a fixed distance?

AJ Yes. It focuses on infinity.

SE Infinity? Does that mean it scans every point?

AJ Yes exactly – it takes about seven months to look at the whole sky.

SE **I still don't understand – if it looks at one point but in infinity...**

AJ **It doesn't look at one point at a given time but at a circle that's about one tenth of a degree across, which is huge. So it takes a very long time. It goes around once a minute, which it does 60 times, and then it moves one twenty-fourth of a degree and does it all over again until – over a period of seven months – it sees the whole sky. Then it does it again and again and again.**

SE **So the actual data you find is light intensities and noise that register as a graph?**

AJ **They come as numbers. It's a big file that's down-loaded from the satellite to us.**

SE **Do these colours, red, blue and green refer to light intensities?**

AJ **Yes. Red is hotter or more intense and blue is less intense. The patterns change much slower than human evolution – if we wait a 100,000 years we might see something small.**

AC **Can you make maps that predict how the universe will change?**

AJ **Yes. But statistically we won't ever see one point again. If we look at the different pictures they're all very homogeneous and similar. That's a hint that the universe started in certain places so if we understand statistically what it's like in one place we can under-stand what it's like in another – like the Milky Way for instance. That's how you do science – you make an observation in one place and assume that observation** tells you about something else. Otherwise it'd be very difficult to do science.

SE **Have you ever looked at Mandala paintings? They're considered maps of the universe. Do you think there is any similarity?**

AJ **In some grand philosophical level there is – we're trying to do a similar thing but have very different methods.**

SE **There was one seminar about those Mandala paintings and I was quite shocked when they told us that we don't live in the centre but in a corner on one island. And you have to go to another island to die. In the centre there was some sort of vacuum indicated by triangles. But is your type of mapping developed to achieve this type of measuring? Or is it developed from a particular applied science?**

AJ **No. I think that with a lot of these things we drive the technology ourselves. The detectors are called bolometers, which are small thermometers.**

SE **Who else uses this technology?**

AJ **I don't know, but they're related to airport scanners that can look at your whole body at once. They have similar frequencies because they're thermo-meters and see different frequencies in heat.**

SE **It's quite interesting how most of the advanced sciences concern data and what you're mapping is what has happened millions of years before. This notion of distance is quite amazing. And the idea of size here is also quite significant – it has something micro-**

cosmic and something abstractly distant in space, scale or time. The work you do is not instant – it's more like a filmstrip in which each point has a different time so that when you put them all together you have a combination of different times. You said it took seven months to record everything but relatively – if you look at the millions of years that light has travelled – the recorded moment probably counts as nothing! Can this technique then also be applied to relatively short distances? Can we scan the unknown surface of the sphere in this room around us or on a city scale?

AJ **It all depends – it's the universe that picks the surface. If you do the same thing in this room the outcome would be very similar to what we see here.**

SE **The machine you use reminds me of radar.**

AJ **Radar is different because it's sending something out and the machines we use only take something in.**

SE **I have something to show you that could be related to geometry. In my recent projects I have been looking at concrete and the fabrication of concrete in certain geometries. They are mostly very simple parabolic formed shapes with mirrored surfaces. The technique is to apply plaster to the surface of soft materials and use it as a mould to cast concrete. From a basic geometric pattern made of these shapes we can make 96 combinations – six multiplied by six multiplied by six. Each component is different but made up from the same repeated patterns. We made wall units like this. Each unit is the same so it can be built up like a puzzle in different directions. We also created furniture that you can configure and connect in different ways and twisted tubes to fit in different ways. I have always** been interested in this kind of thing where you apply certain things in/to a particular environment – something that appears ridiculous or absolutely useless. I find these things the most beautiful. I am equally interested in the principles and technologies of mapping the unknown and then creating models to describe it. But I suppose you see every day completely differently to us architects. I mean when you look at the sky you must see something completely different to our view. It might sound quite naïve but when I hear about these universal things I realise what a short life we have!

AJ I get that as well – but I also think it's amazing that we've figured out all this knowledge and can actually do these experiments. Here we are incredibly finite beings who are able to understand things over 15 billion years old – as far as we know there are no other creatures in the universe that can do this.

AC I have built kinetic structures with moving lamps that shift in a circular motion, like an atmospheric structure coming into being.

AJ Do you show the mechanism in the gallery as well?

AC Yes. With photographs because they allow you to show these mechanical movements during a longer moment and fix those movements. Originally I just wanted to make a kinetic structure but I had to document it and then I noticed that you get these stripes on the photograph made by the lights in the structure – so it shows the same phenomenon in a different way.

AJ That reminds me of one of my animations.

SE I was wondering could we use the data from your machine for the project?

AJ It would be technically possible, but the big problem is privacy – we can't share the data for another couple of years. But what we do have is the data from the last experiments so we have a good approximation of what the data would look like. We really do know what the sky looks like – it's not a simulation. But we wouldn't be able to do this in real time, although that would have been very exciting.

SE One thing that is really nice about this imagery is that we see the inverted image of the universe because the position we have is from a space that doesn't exist for us. The most striking pictures for us are when Apollo sends pictures back to Earth and we see ourselves floating on these spherical images.

AC In a similar but more complicated construction we see three rotational parts. So it's actually a growing model that expands and grows in a spiral manner. I also photographed two sphere-phases on one slide. It's a long exposure for these photographs that are about the disappearing aspect of machines and the image taking its place. I have created five constructions like this.

SE So the strings create their own geometry as the system of strings creates its own variable. It's like a puppet show.

AJ Is it driven by the weight? Or is there an external power?

AC The sticks are moved by a motorised string and the

counter-weights pull it back as the motor moves in an alternate motion.

AJ So here's another interesting thing. It's exactly the same problem as how you make a projection because it's related to the typology. You tile the sphere with bigger parts and it's set up so that every pixel has the same area but can be different shapes depending on where you are in the sphere. This is what we have to do so it's a very difficult mathematical problem. There is no optimum answer – that's part of the problem.

AC It's difficult to compare that to my approach because what I do is quite primitive – making a world map. I use this primitive system because it interested me that the pentagon, which is such a strange shape, allows you to arrange the shapes in a system. But these systems – if you look at them superficially – can seem very distorted.

AJ Do you use a mathematical formula? Perhaps we can apply it to the machine I have and see what it'd look like.

AC I wrote a very primitive program that can calculate these curvatures. I've tried this method on building other spatial entities. Of course the method is not so evident anymore. Another project I did is where I built a small light into a die and it's photographed in the dark so it can leave the trace of the die's movement. So photographing from one point is usually not enough because these objects are moving away form the camera – so I made a multi-view system with mirrors that can follow the object constantly. It's a very big camera that puts six images onto the one slide. Of course every fall of the die is different and so each photograph is different. Another example is where I made a four-metre-high construction with six cameras, which gives a good image quality that I can work with.

AJ **So what shall we build?**

SE **The other teams seem to be more directly related to energy than our topic – 'mechanical'. I do think that our work has quite a lot in common in terms of vocabulary and mechanical interest. I think the idea of scale is quite significant for all of us, we have the artist's scale, my scale – which is architectural – and then we have the infinite scale of the universe. I don't know exactly how we can use this yet so perhaps you could explain what you really specialise in?**

AJ **It's a long story but I'll explain it to you. I'll start by giving you the whole overview and then I'll tell you what I do. Two hundred times a second we get a number and that number goes around the sky. The sky is made up of many galaxies. Everything else is mainly noise and cosmic. We focus on the cosmic for one hour and then in the second hour we will be a little bit further along with maybe some longer or shorter distances in between the lights – similar but not exactly the same. We do this for days on end and then we wrap the outcome back onto the sphere. Everything overlaps and when you wait a long time there's a lot of overlap – especially on the poles – where you cross a lot. On the equator you don't cross very much. You use these crossings to further eliminate the noise because that means every time you pass by you see the exact same thing but from many different perspectives – so you get a clearer image of it. So what we do is take all of this information together with some further infor-mation about the properties of the noise system and it** turns into a very complicated mathematical problem but that's just what it is – a math problem. We then take all this information and start making the map. And this is where it gets a little more complicated because I lied when I said it's only noise + cosmic, it's actually noise + cosmic + instrument because in a way the instrument smears out what it sees and we want to remove that smearing.

SE Do you write the programs for this?

AJ The last 15 years I've spent figuring out how to write these programs because the mathematics isn't easy. But I don't really write the programs myself but I figure out the formulas the program should solve. So then you have the maps and you need to correct the focal points because this only makes sense if you know where the galaxy should be and where it actually ended up. So we have to iterate and correct our model of the instrument based on these results and hope it starts to make sense. So this is where we actually start doing science. This is the general idea – you start from these time strings and you use them to refine your instrument and then you start doing the science from that outcome. We're still in an early stage because we've only been able to see the sky once during the last seven months. Now we have one full map of the sky, which is a quarter of the work we wanted to do. So this is the hard part – the moment you need to understand your instrument very well and you have to keep fixing your understanding of it. So we're still in this early stage but if we are fairly naïve about our analyses of the data it's pretty clear that it will be the best experiment of its kind ever done. The idea is good – so it seems like we're on track.

SE **Are there any other institutions conducting similar experiments?**

AJ **Well this is huge. Just to make it clear this doesn't just involve me – it involves 400 PhDs around the world. There was a previous satellite – the W-Map – that had a different technical approach. It still made the same sort of map but it was a very different kind of experiment. And there is also a whole generation of different experiments that don't take place in space but involve ground-based telescopes or balloons. I'm involved in a couple of these ground-based experiments, which can be a bit more cutting edge. When you put something in space you have to use a decadeold technology that's been proven and there are no questions about whether it'll work of not. On Earth you can experiment.**

AC **That's very interesting. And it makes me think of something else about how someone who analyses economies might look at things in similar ways – in the sense that they map different behaviours and patterns – but the one thing they don't have is a map.**

AJ **Exactly. Because we know the coordinate system and they don't.**

SE **But your analysis – it is an actual product isn't it?**

AJ **Yes.**

SE **I'm just wondering why this map is so important?**

AJ **It's very useful for someone like me because it's the first time I've seen something like it. But there must be some kind of an agenda beyond the mapping? What sort of potential would this mapping have?**

AC **I'm not sure what you mean exactly but it's just basically able to do the science. It can figure out what the early universe was like and what the future universe could be like and how much dark matter there is – it's able to answer all these questions.**

SE **But, for example, can these patterns that light and noise create also be directly related to dark matter?**

AJ **Definitely. If there were no dark matter the patterns we can see here would look very different. I don't know exactly how, but the sizes and differences would be very different. But I haven't explained what I mean by 'doing science'. When you have a relatively expensive stereo, for example, you have a mixer that has these different bars with different frequencies that take the sound and split it up into different frequencies. That means that you are taking a one-dimensional curve and splitting it into these long-wavelengths – the lower notes – and the higher frequencies into the short-wavelength – the high notes. You can assign a number for any particular frequency and that's one dimension. Now it turns out that you cannot only do that in two dimensions but also on a curved surface or over a sphere.**

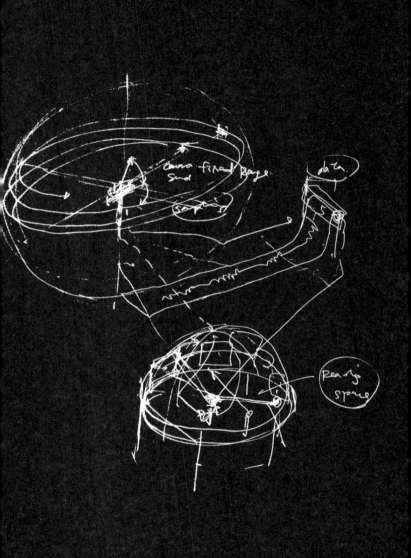

Yet how can one measure the size and quality of a sheer drop in the space in connection with a certain room? How can one measure the quality of Lord Jim's fall when it is a fall from which he will never rise again? How can one measure buildings, if an amphitheatre can become a city, and a theatre a house? ... And for every authentic artist, this means the desire to remake, not in order to effect some changes (which is the mark of superficial people) but out of a strange profundity of feeling for things, in order to see what action develops in the same context, or how, conversely, the context makes slight alterations in the action.

Aldo Rossi,
A Scientific Autobiography

ENERGY AS CONTEXT

STEFANO RABOLLI PANSERA

Context is not a given intervention but the critical definition of a field of forces through which a space is produced and activated. The notion of energy subverts the concept of a homogeneous space–time continuum – with each proposal interacting with its temporal and spatial context. If context actively deforms space then what are the consequences for form? What unexpected ramifications do our actions have on their surroundings? What is the scale of context?

The conventional division of scale from big to small is subverted by the continuous emergence of the very big within the very small. Scale is substituted by resolution and architectural scale performs at a number of different and interlinked levels implying that the impact of the architectural intervention is always somewhere else – simultaneously operating both here and elsewhere.

The electric prototype shows how a small detail – a light bulb – expressed the global scale, while the simple action of switching a light activates an extended infrastructural network. The chemical prototype reveals how the very act of breathing connects different spatial scales from the molecular transformative to the human scale, and the shrinking Arctic glaciers. Reiner de Graaf argues for an appropriate scale for the energetic intervention and claims that the political reorganisation of Europe as a patchwork of energy sources plays a complimentary role. Alessandro Marini describes how land use management is the critical factor in determining how any new development understands a contextual transition from the local to the global. And Stefano Boeri observes how the city and natural and cultivated areas can be seen as hybrid territories that are like fragments of a kaleidoscope in continuous movement.

ALESSANDRO MARINI

LOCAL →TO→ GLOBAL

Energy use is a global issue that requires a global solution. At the operative level, however, the local scale is vital for two reasons. Any action has to be manageable and workable in the territory involved. And any territory can have different outcomes, solutions and opportunities according to its history and economic development. Land use management is the most critical factor in determining a new development model focused on a better use of scale that takes account of the contextual transition from local to global.

The contemporary European landscape looks like an enormous kaleidoscope, one in which the city, nature and agricultural areas are no longer easily identifiable but have been compromised through a series of annexations and crossovers that have completely transformed the image of a landscape divided into discrete sections.

BAUKUH, ALBERTO GARUTTI, LUCA CELARDO

Energy cannot be stored – it must be produced moment by moment, second by second. If a large amount of energy is required at any specific moment then more energy must be introduced into the system, leading to a continuous balancing between the supply. In Italy the management of this network follows economic and geopolitical regulations that govern the various territories. The electrical feed at Fondazione Cini is supplied from a dense network of energy exchange based at Sacca Fisola, which in turn is fed by Veneto and Fruili Venezia Giulia, Emilia Romagna, and the gas-powered thermal power stations of Torviscosa, Marghera Azotati, Turnigo, Chivasso, Porto Viro – all of which are themselves linked through a network of gas supplies to sources in Algeria, Russia, Libya, the Netherlands and Norway. The coal-fired power plants of Marghera, Fusina, Genoa and North Torrevaliga Brindisi are supplied with coal from the mines of South Africa, Indonesia, Colombia, Russia, Venezuela and China. The oil-powered plants of Piombino, Montalto di Castro, San Filippo, Fiume Santo and Monfalcone draw on pipelines from Russia, Libya, Saudi Arabia, Iran and Iraq. Finally, wind turbines and the hydroelectric stations in Somplago, Cavilla and Barga bring together Puglia and Sicily.

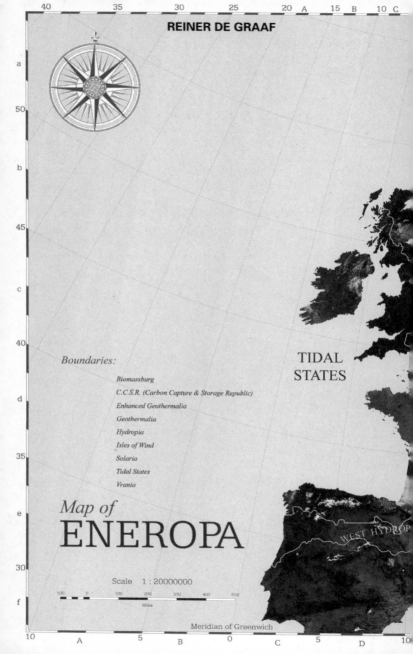

TIDAL
STATES

Boundaries:

Biomassburg

C.C.S.R. (Carbon Capture & Storage Republic)

Enhanced Geothermalia

Geothermalia

Hydropia

Isles of Wind

Solaria

Tidal States

Vrania

Map of
ENEROPA

WEST HYDROP

Scale   1 : 20000000

100   0   100   200   300   400   500
Miles

Meridian of Greenwich

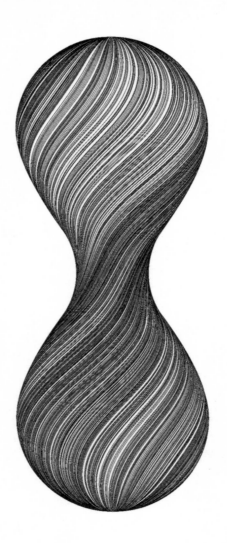

CHEMICAL ENERGY
Territorial Agency, Amanda Chatten, Nina Canell

Given the essentially invisible nature of most chemical transactions we chose to focus our investigation on the virtually imperceptible fabric of Earth's atmosphere – air. The socio-spatial implications of air are perhaps most explicitly demonstrated in its action as a carrier of the photosynthetic process. This exhibition presents the research project at three scales – the atomic (the moment electrons change in chemical energy transformation), the human (the act of breathing) and the territorial (the spatial transformations induced by climate and atmospheric changes).

Taking photosynthesis and the act of breathing as a point of departure we initiated a conversation regarding the spatial, political and economic distribution of air and asked such questions as 'What is sovereignty without inhabitation?' We also elaborated on the implications of the dream of using oxygen as a catalyst for heightened consciousness and outlined the nature of chemical changes at the molecular level.

Operating at the extremes of the material and immaterial world this work was presented in three forms – a drawing of the atomic nature of chemical change in the atmosphere, an enclosed object in which the oxygen level was increased by five per cent and a large polyptych that illustrated our exploration of the geopolitical transformations in the global north.

Amanda Chatten **You can only see chemical energy when it's transformed into life or another form. For example solar radiation can be turned into chemical energy but you can only see it when it does things. Does that actually make the title of this project 'When Energy becomes Form' redundant?**

Nina Canell **Well plants and animals are energy also becoming form, but that's perhaps slightly superficial.**

Territorial Agency **What is entropy in terms of chemical energy?**

AC **Entropy is the tendency towards disorder so if you have two solutions and you combine them together they generally don't remain two layers, they intermix. This increases the disorder.**

TA **Because entropy is the product of a reaction?**

AC **Entropy is a measure of the level of disorder in a system. Imagine you've got two boxes of black and white ping-pong balls and you put them together, when they're separate they have a lower measure of entropy than when they're mixed. It has to do with the number of ways of arranging things – the more ways you can arrange something, the higher the level of entropy.**

TA **In relation to that can we talk about questions of juxtaposition and aggregation such as informal semantics?**

NC **Is it the higher the entropy, the higher the amount of disorder and the more combinations there could be? So when you bring in the notion of juxtaposition together with those possible combinations of things** and people, is it good to have entropy?

AC The natural tendency is for entropy to increase.

TA But that goes against bureaucracy!

NC Could the archive be a suitable topic to work around?

AC No. An archive is a very ordered system so it has less entropy.

TA So nature tries to make everything more disorderly and humans try to order everything, which results in our society. But our project doesn't necessarily have to do with the chemical does it?

AC Well some other words that came up were 'resistance' and 'juxtaposition' and I'm interested in this bounce between nature and culture. Maybe in a more material way than you two would in your work but...

TA I think we could probably use chemical energy as a way of thinking about transformation. It might not sound very open at this point but it could be if we steer it in this direction.

NC So we can only consider chemical energy when it turns into something else?

AC Or through a rearrangement or transformation.

NC Is a bomb chemical energy, for example?

AC It is stored chemical energy that becomes heat and sound.

TA **And is sound a part of that energy? Is sound actually energy?**

AC **Yes. It's a wave that stores energy and sound is dissipated by being transformed into chemical energy when the wave motion is transferred to the bonds in the molecule, which makes it vibrate more. That makes it heat up a little bit and that's how sound dissipates.**

TA **So where does the energy go with sound?**

AC **It physically squashes the air.**

TA **What I'm interested in is exactly the situation we now find ourselves in: what kind of space is it that brings people together to work on things. How can we sustain this? Architects are always interested in finding out about this space and how we can design it in a way that allows things to happen. To go back to the idea of sound: the chemical bond is transformed through the addition of heat. So you add chemical energy to the bond?**

AC **You spark the reaction, yes.**

NC **So it becomes unstable and produces heat again and with it sound. And the sound pushes the bullet at high speeds on the way to killing someone. Even so the overall amount of energy stays the same?**

AC **Yes. Energy is always conserved.**

NC **How much energy is there in the universe? Or don't we know this?**

AC **I think we know because we know that $E = MC^2$ and**

what the value of M must be.

NC Do you know the mass of the universe?

AC I think they must do and how much dark energy and dark matter must be out there.

NC I thought the universe was infinite!

AC The universe might be but matter isn't. So that means the amount of mass and the amount of energy isn't infinite.

NC So we are this little planet and we get all this energy and it's transformed into chemical energy through a synthesis – not only photosynthesis.

AC No. We use metabolism, which is a sort of inverse version of photosynthesis to create all the other structures in our bodies.

NC But without photosynthesis we wouldn't exist?

AC That's right. It begins with photosynthesis.

NC And how can photosynthesis happen? You need CO_2: but was CO_2 present in the atmosphere at the beginning?

AC I'm not entirely sure, but it must have been! You get CO_2 with volcanoes and when the earth was very young it was very volcanic so there would have been an awful lot of CO_2 released.

NC And CO_2 is transformed by solar radiation, which is a form of heat?

AC Solar radiation is created by light photons, which are little packets of energy.

TA Are these photons electromagnetic? Do they disappear with the solar wind, and that somehow becomes the Northern Lights and other such phenomena?

NC We could do an artificial Northern Lights! They also make sound...

TA I think Galileo gave the Aurora Borealis its name because it gave out a long red light that was visible all the way to Italy. But both trees and plants and bombs or combustion engines are driven by chemical energy. A combustion engine works because it uses hydrocarbons and oxygen, which comes from the plants, so basically the oil that we burn in a car is a dead store of solar energy. Is it the transformation of one form of potential energy?

AC It contains chemical potential.

NC So the plant transforms solar energy into chemical energy and when it dies that energy is stored. Then we tap into it by burning it and that further adds oxygen and energy – it wouldn't work without adding energy.

AC Exactly. You have to start the process by adding energy and once it starts it releases more energy.

NC Is this the main process of chemical energy that humans use? Burning things?

AC Yes. That's also what our bodies do. And that's what fire does. Fire is chemical energy – it releases heat and light.

NC **We should make a fire!**

TA **No. We should make a forest. It's easy to make a plantation but how could we make a forest?**

NC **When wood has been burned what's actually left?**

AC **The wood hasn't completely burned you are left with carbon. If you have a complete combustion you're left with CO_2 and water.**

NC **What do you think of in terms of your practice as an architect when you think of a prototype?**

TA **A prototype is really just an idea.**

NC **So we could make a forest! How do we make a forest? I would like to make a forest!**

AC **Forests are different all over the world: it's highly dependent on the environment.**

TA **How do you make a human forest? I mean we're not plants, plants can make their own forest. We could do some research into the specific areas around Venice and see if we can find something interesting in relation to forests. Architects are always dealing with how to shape cities and things like that. Basically what we're trying to do is make human forests where people adapt to their environment rather than respond entropically. Does a forest have a lot of entropy?**

AC **No. Forests are usually complexly ordered. It's only when that order breaks down and the complex molecules break down completely that you have a lot of entropy.**

TA Is that what we mean when we say 'beyond entropy'? When it's broken down?

NC Entropy is always there – it's a measure. That would be like saying you want to go 'beyond temperature'.

AC Entropy isn't something you can get away from. It's always there, it's intrinsic.

NC I would like to get beyond gravitation. Or make a mini forest.

TA How do we get light?

NC From the sun. Is that what makes forests different: the amounts of light they receive?

AC It's temperature, amount of water and the type of soil.

NC The amount of light. In the north, for example, there isn't much light and so they have different types of forest.

AC Exactly. The trees aren't so wasteful and they don't throw away their leaves every year!

NC So why are the trees in the north similar to the trees in the high mountains? Is it only a question of temperature?

AC And water.

NC It's why you get very tall trees that reach up to the light. So if we build our forest on top of a mountain we wouldn't need so much light.

TA There's a chemical city in Venice – Mestre – that lies on the mainland and is one of the biggest chemical plants in Italy. It's very toxic. It's a place where it's possible for humans to tap into the chemical energy from oil and ammonia and create a range of chemical products such as plastics. That's almost all dismantled now, but at the same time the city of Venice has become less and less inhabited and more about tourism. So Venice is becoming progressively unbalanced and there is no longer a constant maintenance of the city. The part local Venetians live in is quite an ugly and uninteresting city. And the chemical city is abandoned. They also have a lot of problems because the river comes in to the city and it's a very fragile environment. It could be interesting to start thinking about what would happen if the three cities started talking to each other instead of having artists, architects and scientists talking to each other.

NC They don't have forests in Venice, though.

TA No, the trees were cut down to make ships. But this is chemical energy – it's storage of chemical energy. Something else completely. Is there something such as artificial life or don't we have that yet?

AC No, that doesn't exist yet. It would be good if our project could reflect something of what we do but I think this thing, 'life', should be present in it because chemical reactions drive life. It's very difficult to think of one thing that could embody that because the micro-scale is actually bond breaking and making and the catalyst to how things change and form. That could also be shown in a graphic way.

NC Can we see the micro-scale?

AC **You can use microscopes to see individual atoms but all you see is little dots and that's why we draw representations.**

NC **What about plasma? What is it exactly – a phase of matter?**

AC **Yes. You have solid, liquid, gas and plasma.**

NC **In relation to chemical energy what happens when there is a phase transition into chemical energy? When water becomes ice – for example – there is no chemical energy involved in that transformation. It's just the molecules behaving in a different way.**

AC **They are kinetic energy changes. Their freedom to move changes but only in terms of one molecule to another beside it, the change doesn't happen within the molecule itself. So it's not a chemical energy transformation. The textbook definition of chemical energy refers to the energy stored within the bonds between atoms.**

NC **How would you show chemical energy in a banal way? It's easy to show kinetic energy, you can demonstrate how it works, but chemical energy can only be written about. We can't see it unless it becomes a plant.**

AC **Or unless the structure changes and it changes colour or shape.**

NC **Exactly. I'm sure there are ways to visualise these phenomena. I think there's something quite poetic about the fact that this is an invisible transformation in a way. I think we should try and use that. From my point of view that is a very interesting element.**

AC **I agree. In the work you showed us many things that were not quite there.**

NC **I sometimes use audio frequencies that are just outside the human hearing range. In working a lot with visual material I think it's very intriguing to think about where the human perception ends and the so-called relational space and things that can happen in the invisible spectrum.**

TA **Do you ever deal with chemical energy in your work?**

AC **Well you're absorbing light that is stored as chemical energy before being released again as light of a different colour. We turn that light into electricity at the edges. So it does go through chemical energy at different stages. If you take a material that absorbs sunlight, for example, then the light is stored within the material as chemical energy. As the molecule is rearranged, long wavelength light is emitted, so it passes through chemical energy. But I think people think of what I do as dealing with light and packets of photons.**

TA **If a photon touches the glass and the glass doesn't have any chemical energy then it doesn't add to its chemical energy? What is the moment when it becomes chemical energy?**

AC **Well if we have nano-crystals in the glass then it transforms.**

TA **So you actually change life when you transform light. But it's not a photosynthetic transformation?**
AC **No. It's more like a transitional state.**

TA **How long does that state last?**

AC It depends on the material. It can be nano- to micro-seconds depending on material. This is all definitely on a very small scale! Because there's such a quick turna-round, time and space are incredibly compressed.

TA Why do you need colour on your panels? Why do you need yellow?

AC The colour you see is actually the light that's being emitted. Generally when you look at something the colour you see is the light that's not absorbed – different materials absorb different parts of the light spectrum.

NC So what you are saying is that the material absorbs the light, which in this case is glass, and you're trying to tap into that?

AC We simply use the absorption and subsequent re-emission of the light as a way of trapping and collect-ing it.

TA So you tap the light and turn it into electric energy.

AC Exactly – from solar to chemical to electrical.

NC How can we see the chemical part?

AC The chemical part occurs when the light is absorbed by the material and excites it and creates more move-ment between the molecules. But it's very difficult to explain.

NC You mentioned that this process is not photo-electric but photovoltaic – what's the difference?

AC With photo-electricity, when you hit a material

electrons are kicked out. Whereas photovoltaic involves an absorption of light that creates electric ampere which stay inside the material and travel to the electrodes.

NC But when light hits the material is that a photoelectric moment?

AC No. That's absorption. Different atoms have a different electrostatic potential and you need a molecule that can oscillate in phase with the light and allow that energy to be transferred from the light into the molecule. For this to happen these components have to be in phase with one another.

TA And then that energy is trapped into a photovoltaic material. Do you need to transfer that to a diode?

AC The photovoltaic material is a diode that allows the electrons to be separated.

NC Where is the chemical energy in the system?

AC It's at the point where the light is absorbed but the electrons have yet to be separated from one another. Where you have this excited state it consists of light coupling with the oscillation of the electric field. But it's incredibly difficult to explain!

TA It's very funny because I think both the visual domain and architects think of order in different ways. So when you say it's disordered we think of simple or complex geometric disorder. But what you're pointing out here is the process of the transformation of energy. A city might seem quite ordered, for example, but it's actually more disordered in terms of systems that use energy. If a forest works well it has a high order but a city doesn't work like that. We should increase the order of a city and reduce the level of entropy. The way in which we use energy should be more ordered.

AC **Why?**

TA **The process of this energy should be more ordered because that's when life can flourish. That's why we'll do a forest!**

NC **Are there experiments that show more than chemical reaction inside glass?**

AC **No. You just see it in the change of colour of the light. It's absorbing the sunlight and emitting it in another colour and that's the embodiment of the transformation. The chemical bit always stays invisible. Entropy is just such a big subject. It's so open, our prototype could be anything from a picture of a molecule, or the bonds between atoms or you could have people sitting in a garden munching on food! It's a massive topic. How can we narrow it down?**

TA **The garden is interesting in relation to order and disorder because it has to be ordered to function but at the same time it's cultivated by humans as opposed to nature. Maybe we should think somewhere in between garden and forest.**

AC **We could also have a growing molecule. Or a plant that grows so fast that you can actually see it grow!**

NC **That could be one kind of chemical transformation: things growing. But how does growth actually happen?**

AC It's cell division. It's a very complex chemical process that consists of burning sugars and rebuilding molecules, including the replication of the DNA.

NC If a forest is an ecosystem what is an ecosystem of chemical energy?

AC The whole planet.

TA We're trying to transfer one practice into another but what if we produce a forest – an ecosystem of practices – in which we all do our thing and profit from one another. We'll have to negotiate because I'm interested in making the forest as a space for negotiation, a political space and a space you inhabit. When you negotiate you give up things. I think that could be an interesting point at which to enter a discussion on the transfer from one form of energy to another and one form of practice into another. The space of negotiation is one in which you both lose something in order to get something else. So when a chemical bomb negotiates with say, electrical radiation, what does it give up?

AC It gives up its current configuration.

TA Exactly – in order to get something else. So there is a transformation. The only way to transform is through a loss of form, so it's a question of loss.

NC It is a question of loss but there is also a new space created through each form of collaboration.

TA Chemical energy can only manifest itself the moment it's transformed into something else and that's equivalent to the moment we meet, when our practices become visible to each other and we give up something as we negotiate. So this is organisational entropy! You progress as a group by losing things individually. If there's going to be a form of entropy then – sorry to be so physical about this – the sum of what you gain will be less than what you lose.

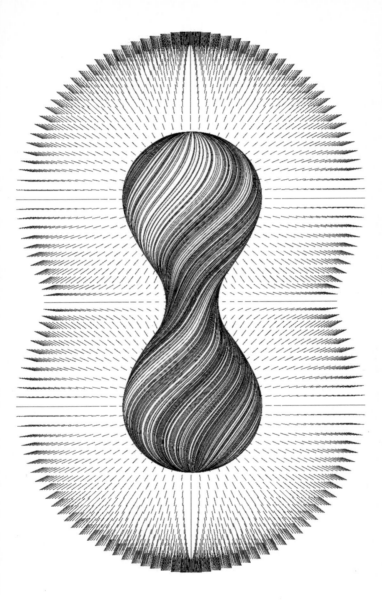

*Not in purism but in the unlimited
contamination of things, of
correspondences, does silence
return. The drawing can be
suggestive, for as it limits
it also amplifies memory, objects,
events. A design pursues this
fabric of connections, memories,
images, yet knowing that in the
end it will have to be definitive
about this or that solution; on
the other hand, the original,
whether in its true or presumed
state will be an obscure object
which is identified with its copy.
Even technique seems to stop at
a threshold where its discipline
dissolves.*

Aldo Rossi,
A Scientific Autobiography

ENERGY AS REPRESEN-TATION

STEFANO RABOLLI PANSERA

The notion of representation is related to the modes we use to represent and communicate space to an audience of potential users. Representation is intimately related to form and scale. How can we represent a space–time event? How can we represent a form that simultaneously exists both here and elsewhere? How can space–time events be communicated, distributed and perceived? What kind of platform can we use to disseminate this information? And what is representation when producers and receivers coincide?

Energy pushes our techniques of representing and communicating space to the extreme. Holographic techniques and serial copying are some of the tools that embody temporality within the representation of spatial events but the dissemination of represenation must consider both the production of information and the audience. Belief systems, collective hallucinations, misinformation and a lack of comprehension seem to be the main devices for the circulation of content and representation of space.

The gravitational prototype uses a forensic technique to unfold the timelines of complex and multivalent events compressed within holographic images. The thermal prototype uses copying as a tool to test energy consumption and measure the level of entropy in serial production. Francesco Garutti explores the notion of secrecy in binding the author and their audience and creating the tension between the spatial and intellectual representations. Joel Newman considers the opportunity that extreme digital compression offers for producing video art. Aaron Levy uses entropy as a curatorial method to trigger unsupervised dialogues that deny any sense of finality or resolution. Finally Christian von Düring represents energy through a literal correspondence to its monetary value.

JOEL NEWMAN

Each minute of every day over 24 hours of video is uploaded to YouTube. More content is generated over a 60-day period than the American television networks have created in over 60 years of broadcasting. **Through Random Access Memory**, the filmmaker Malcolm Le Grice writes, 'the establishment of non-linear access – sequentiality – is replaced by non-linear code, addressing the potential to massively extend the flex-ibility of data recovery and combination'. The technology Le Grice is describing is not only essential to online video server technologies that draw on all aspects of human existence but also to digital or non-linear video editing systems. Luckily we do not function like YouTube in indiscriminately gathering as much data as possible – instead our subconscious instincts filter out extraneous material and we are left with the necessary remnants. Recently a number of video artists – who explore the medium through **Glitch Art** – have rejected the notion of a perfect technical memory-recall in favour of wondering at the unexpected beauty technological accidents bring about.

It could be said that the idea of 'perpetual peace' in Immanuel Kant's time had a relatively high degree of entropy – not unlike that of a string of random letters. In a period characterised by socio-political tensions that defy simple solutions, curators must respond to this reality by acknowledging uncertainty, ambiguity and confusion. By acknowledging – in short – 'entropy'. The value of embracing entropy as a curatorial methodology will not only be judged in such measured outcomes as exhibitions or events with fixed durations, but also through unsupervised dialogues that continue beyond our supervision and foreclose any sense of finality or resolution.

The seemingly straightforward gesture of staging a series of questions could offer another pathway to the otherwise fraught role of the contemporary curator, providing an alternative to the pageantry of prevailing dogmatic approaches. Not to 'display' art or architecture in any conventional sense – or call attention to oneself and one's practice – but to actively seek out entropic variables such as peace and generate projects around them. To create the conditions for conversation about problems and concepts that are without a single solution. And to move a conversation in different directions with multiple partners. Kant's openness to ideas and his embrace of entropy constitutes for us another way forward, another curatorial approach in the face of the uncertainties in which we live.

Perpetual Peace

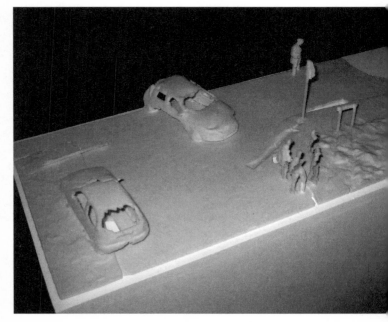

Bodies are movements that slowly coalesce into form. Form emerges from a **diagram of forces** and we can therefore read its history. Energy registers in the shape of things. The past history of a body **then** and the larger space around it **there** are folded into its configuration **now.** Matter makes its own record in space and evolution in time. This is the forensic impetus behind form-making and form-reading. It can be applied both on a planetary scale as astronomers reconstruct the chronology of impacts on the moon by looking at the pattern of overlapping craters, and also on a smaller scale as police investigators can read a bullet hole to find information about the ballistic trajectory of a bullet through space. It is the unfolding of an event-history. Other forensic scientists build 3D models of a crime scene or accident to reconstruct the sequence of events. This prototype explores this **holographic** side of matter and energy. It investigates the holographic principle as it can be applied to history. When these images are scanned and **printed** in 3D matter, we can accurately and originally reproduce a documentary object or a documentary sculpture. This presentation therefore aims to present a series of prototypes of documentary object or sculpture as a potential tool for investigating history as a gravitational practice. In our project, spatial and material information become an entry point to reconstruct timelines of complex and multivalent events.

FRANCESCO GARUTTI

The construction of secrecy in an artwork creates a tension between the work and its audience. Over the last decade several artists have explored this possibility both through the contents of their work and the increasingly obscure, hidden, and intentionally lateral ways in which it can be distributed – modes that generate a kind of gravitational energy which puts the work and audience into play. Disinformation should be seen as a possibility and a mode of producing – as Jacques Derrida has asserted – infinite contexts, multiple interpretations and parallel mindscapes. Transparency does not ensure the future legibility of any work and a number of contemporary artists consider opacity as more valuable than transparency.

The work of Pawel Althamer constitutes not so much an aesthetic system as a system of collective beliefs and hallucinations that attract and absorb viewers. This attraction consists of a sort of magnetism that relies on small objects or even non-objects. Althamer's work 'Path' can only be seen as a slender trace that emanates from the map of the exhibition and begins in a park where the other works were displayed. The path is unpaved like any other route in the park and there are no texts or captions to describe the work. Visitors are encouraged to walk along a path that continues for kilometres amidst the greenery. Some people only walk a part of it, others not at all, while others still will continue all the way to the end where it simply stops on the outskirts of the city. Only those who allow themselves to be guided to the end of the path can know something more of its intent.

CHRISTIAN VON DÜRING

What is the Value of Energy? 2010

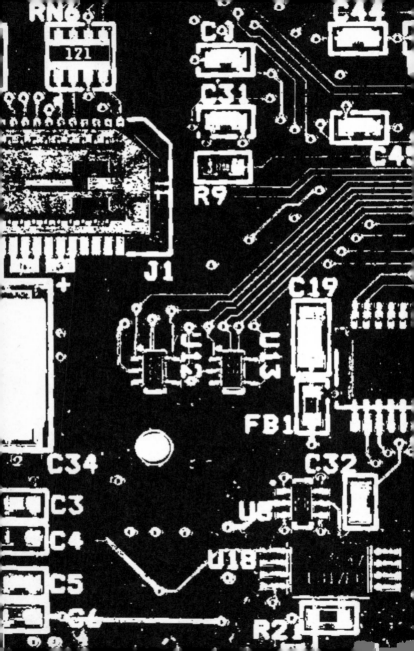

THERMAL ENERGY
Dave Clements, Wilfredo Prieto, Ines Weizman

Recently 3D printers and scanners have become a challenge to conventional methods of manufacturing and distributing goods. With its capacity to manufacture complicated and intricate forms a 3D printer suggests a prototype with which to examine energy consumption and entropy through the deviation of form in serial production. Equally the precision opened up by the pairing of a 3D scanner and 3D printer also allows for new possibilities of reproduction or – literally – copying. Similar to the early discussions on the development of photography, the notion of the authentic and unique artwork is once again held in suspense and invites intensive questioning. This project deals with questions of entropy through printing technology.

3D printing technology complicates the problem of mechanical reproduction, as it not only concerns the product but also the machine, which can potentially reproduce its own parts. Our exhibition considers the construction of a machine – a 3D printer – that has been conceived as a form of mimicry or forgery with an emphasis on its 'performativity' and the reproduction of the original trying to be 'imitate[d] with obsessive care.' Similar to a copying laboratory – and intensifying the pleasurable rituals of learning, familiarisation and invention – drawings and animations of the existing machine's individual elements were produced and explored in respect to their function and form with the intention to replicate the machine.

Dave Clements **From my point of view as a physicist –
at a very basic level energy doesn't transform. Take
the example of gravitational energy – when you drop
something down a hill it will lose potential energy.
At the same time it will gain kinetic energy and then
when it hits the bottom all that energy will transform
into heat. At some point in all this you have thermal
energy – a waste energy – as it's very difficult for thermal energy to transform into anything else. That would
be like pushing the ball back up the hill. Of course you
can do that if you try hard. You could do it if you have
two things at different temperatures – one hotter and
one colder. You take the hotter one and bring it to the
same temperature as the colder one, making something in the middle do the work. Something useful.
Think of a steam train where you have a hot furnace
that is hotter than everything outside it. You use the
furnace to boil water, generating steam and pressure
to drive the train. So there is a chemical energy in the
wood fuel – a 'potential' energy that connects energies. But then you are confronted with friction and the
train will need to go back to a normal heat again if you
want to stop the wheels at some point. Here we are
getting to the formal definition of entropy and its relation with thermodynamics – to how engines work and
heat up. It's all very basic physics and could be seen
as my starting point for this project. A practical example is a heat engine called the Sterling engine, which
allows you to transform difference in temperature into
a form of mechanical energy. As long as you have a
heating source you can do something and you can
wrap any story around it – for example, the heat being
generated by burning capital tells a political story.
There are many other stories you could come up with.**

Ines Weizman **In relation to this project I am wondering how our fields of practice relate? And what kinds of speciality to look for? Because there is a more theoretical field besides the practical one that you address – energy is a very abstract term. There is a lot of meaning with this term and spaces related to it, so what could we come up with? You say a machine – that's very technical.**

DC **Well I am a scientist.**

IW **I also look at movement and repetition in my work. One of the images I showed specifically dealt with repetition – it's a construction of a replica building that was never built. It's a building that exists in our fantasies – the dream of architects. You know the building? It's like things students would always invest themselves in, study, make models of and generate detailed sections. The interesting thing about this building is that it has a swimming pool on the first floor. It was imagined by the architect – it's almost like a love letter through architecture.**

DC **I don't know the history of this building.**

IW **During the 1920s the Paris intelligentsia were fascinated by Josephine Baker, the African-American dancer who performed wild dances while wearing banana-skirts but not much else. She fascinated the architect Adolf Loos, who he saw several performances. At a party she said to him – 'You know, I'm looking for an architect'. And he said – 'Why did you not tell me? I'm the best architect in the world!' This is all we really know about what happened, and he finally designed that villa for her. It is all about creative energy. For me, I got this very strange invitation to build a series of 100 villas in Mongolian China in the middle of the Gobi desert.**

DC **It's like what's happening in Dubai with the building of those new islands.**

IW **Exactly. Terrible neo-liberal projects that create dispersed communities. For me it was important in terms of energy – how much creative energy did we want to bring to this project? We were confronted with not knowing the rules of creativity. The Chinese wanted Western architects to be creative and show their dreams. By introducing the idea of the replica I eliminated that element and the project moved more into the area of copyright, which is a kind of plagiarism. That's something that fascinates me and might relate to entropy.**

DC **Yes. Entropy and information are very related.**

IW **I think it's about not constantly producing the new or thinking in linear ways. We can also regain energies that are already present.**

Wilfredo Prieto **It is possible to start imagining something in between both your topics. You know the Ecosphere – the NASA invention? It's an enclosed ecosystem. We say that one element contains it all. It's an example where the life is continuous – a beautiful truth in both its idea and in its generation. You have many forms of human energy and one of them is making money and all that. In the case of the Ecosphere there's only one moving cycle, which is not going in any other direction. It remains static. And it's aesthetic at the same time. But I'm not sure if there's a relation to real life. Does it have a normal socio-political or general concept? Or functionality? Imagine the idea of searching for energy all for nothing. It reminds me of the perpetual mobile. I love this idea because for many years there were people looking for this.**

DC **They still do.**

WP **Is this invention actually possible?**

DC **No, it's completely impossible. But there are still people who put out adverts on websites. 'Free imagery of perpetual motion machines'. The shady words they use to get around it are terms like 'thermodynamics'. There is not enough energy – there's a limit to everything – that's basically what thermodynamics says. You can't win and you can't break even and everything you do increases entropy. Another word often used by these perpetual motion people is 'zero-point-energy' – but how can this be a concept in counter mechanics? The energy of the vacuum? To make certain equations work within counter mechanics you don't look at the absolute volumes of energy, you just look at the differences. To solve this sum you take two numbers for the equation and you literally subtract the infinity from it. That infinity has been labelled zero-point-energy. So with everything we do we're looking at fluctuations above wherever the zero-point-energy is. This means that the zero-point-energy could be absolutely nothing at all or it could be an extremely large number. And those radical free energy people will probably tell you that at some level you get a very high number. They will say that their perpetual motion machine is giving you zero-point energy so it is free energy. It's all nonsense – but it doesn't stop people.**

IW **I'm trying to think again of the perpetual mobile as a more conceptual idea. We could try to research an actual scientific model, such as those of the seventeenth century where alchemists tried to gain energy. This will force us to understand what they're attempting to do. A meeting point between our practices could be the** development of a fake physics. The machine that we develop with it should already be invented. The model should also be invented already – such as a Leonardo Da Vinci flying machine. Let's go back to one of those origins and really study it.

DC There are a number of people I know who are interested in medieval technology and the history of technology in a slightly jokey way.

IW I guess that the further you go back the simpler or less machine-like technology is. It would be very interesting to look at early experiments in energy.

DC Yes. It probably is much simpler – they are all made with wood and string. It reminds me of where I started off. Would it be possible to make a Sterling cycle engine with medieval technology? With glass, and maybe copper or lead pipe and wood? I will have to see what actually goes into a Sterling cycle engine.

IW I'm slightly hesitant about the work we presented last night. We had a lot of machines and I'm not sure if I want that. I think it's important to go back to an experiment. A scientific experiment doesn't necessarily need to be the kind of experiment where you put something in here and it steams out there and then something moves. It's about maintaining regularity in the experiment – I really wonder if we could gain something from regularity.

DC We could make a work that requires greater participation. So that whoever is looking at it actually has to take part by doing the experiment – by pressing a button for instance.

IW I really enjoyed the scientist's talks that were quite abstract and almost incomprehensible for the others – as if there was a limit even though the topic had already been reduced to 'space'. It was so interesting to see how there was an entirely other world of meaning among architects and artists, even though there is a point where we all meet. What I mean is that it cannot only be the machine and energy where our different fields meet. Through this collaboration we can attempt to produce some sort of result.

DC It's more about making an experience rather than a result.

IW Exactly. That is what we should present. I'm not sure what the outcome will be – or what the prototype could be.

DC Or what manner of presentation we should use.

DC Exactly. I think the main thing is to just understand it and to understand each other. That's the project.

DC That's not such a bad idea.

IW I can speak about entropy a little bit more comfortably and you know a little bit more about the kind of world we're in at the moment.

DC And you can add some historical elements from the East and you can add some from Cuba. From a political point of view both Eastern Europe and Cuba had to deal with very different problems.

WP Yes – completely different problems.

IW We could make a sugar machine. Cuba sold sugar to the whole Soviet Union.

WP They don't do that any longer.

IW It's more a gesture. The Soviets needed sugar and Cuba had to give something but they had nothing really to give – so they sent sugar. On top of all this sugar is the energy for the human body.

DC Sugar burns very nicely.

WP It's very symbolic.

IW And it tastes good. When you heat it up and it caramelises, it also gives a very nice surface.

DC If you take icing sugar and grind it very finely and mix it with the air in a specific way you can also make it explosive. It's always good to have some pyrotechnics.

IW I like pyrotechnics. It's also perfect for Venice.

DC Yes. Thinking of Venice, it's such a medieval city – a perfect site for going back to clockwork and alchemy.

WP I think it sounds very good because the beginning is very open now. There are so many possibilities!

Image courtesy: Dave Clements, Wilfredo Prieto, Ines Weizman

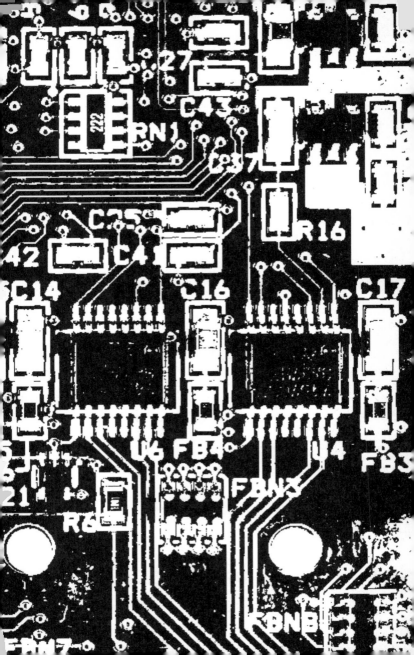

APPENDIX

Beyond Entropy: When Energy Becomes Form
is a two-year research programme promoted by the
Architectural Association and defined by the pursuit of
new paradigms in the relationship between energy and
space. The first phase of the programme consisted of
a series of lectures at the AA featuring Giovanni Anc-
eschi, Massimo Bartolini, David Claerbout, Martin Creed,
Wilfredo Prieto, Vid Stojevic and Roberto Trotta, while
its core developed out of a collaboration between eight
teams of artists, architects and scientists on eight specific forms of energy:

Chemical Energy
Nina Canell
Amanda Chatten
Territorial Agency

Mechanical Energy
Shin Egashira
Andrew Jaffe

Mass
Rubens Azevedo
Ariel Schlesinger
Vid Stojevic

Gravitational Energy
Peter Coles
Eyal Weizman

Electric Energy
baukuh
Giuseppe Celardo
Alberto Garutti

Potential Energy
Peter Liversidge
Julian Loeffler
Roberto Trotta

Thermal Energy
Dave Clements
Wilfredo Prieto
Ines Weizman

Sound
Massimo Bartolini
Dario Benedetti
Riccardo Rossi
Salottobuono

After an initial visit to CERN in Geneva, the various
teams built a series of specific prototypes that questioned the conventional relationship between energy
and form. The development of these prototypes hap-

pened simultaneously in several European locations: Paris, London, Berlin, Milan and Barcelona.

In August 2010 the prototypes were then exhibited at the Fondazione Giorgio Cini as part of the collateral events of the 12th International Architecture Biennale in Venice. Coinciding with the opening of the Biennale, a symposium broadened the field of research even further. The 11-hour event gathered together international speakers such as Hans Ulrich Obrist, Reiner de Graaf, Toni Negri, Charles Jencks, Matteo Pasquinelli and Ricky Burdett.

The final exhibition of the updated prototypes took place at the Architectural Association in May 2011.

BIOGRAPHIES

Rubens Azevedo graduated from the AA in 2002. He has worked at Foster + Partners, taught Diploma Unit 3 at the AA with Pascal Schöning, collaborated with Shin Egashira, designed several unbuilt houses, made several films and participated in exhibitions. He is the co-editor of the book *Cinematic Architecture* and is currently working at JH Architecture.

Massimo Bartolini is an Italian-born artist whose work embraces various materials and techniques, from sculpture and performance to photography. His works induce in the viewer a meditative state that is still highly experiential, reflecting on the relativity of what is stable and unchangeable.

baukuh is an architectural office founded in 2004. No member of baukuh is ever individually responsible for any project which goes out from the office. In order to work together without a hierarchical structure and without a stylistic dogma, baukuh developed a rational and explicit design method. This method is based on the critical de-coding of the architecture of the past and on the logical re-coding of this knowledge into contemporary design. The knowledge encoded in the architecture of the past is public. Starting from this heritage it is possible to solve every architectural problem.

Dario Benedetti has a MSc in Civil Engineering and a PhD in Materials Engineering from the University of Brescia, where he is currently working as a researcher on the use and development of innovative analytical techniques applied to archaeometry and conservation science. In 2006, 2007 and 2009 he worked in the Department of Scientific Research at the Metropolitan Museum of New York as a research scholar. He is founder of START Solutions and Technologie.

Nina Canell is an artist whose installations present themselves as a series of sculptural interludes that question the reliability and fixity of physical forms. An improvisational methodology and a flexibility of form highlight Canell's quest for sculpture, which exists somewhere between an event and an object, addressing our empirical understanding and willingness to engage with multiple and complex readings.

Giuseppe Celardo graduated in Physics at Pavia University and completed his PhD at Milan University. He worked as a postdoc at the Los Alamos National Laboratory (Los Alamos, USA), at the University of Puebla BUAP (Mexico) and at Tulane University (New Orleans, USA). He was originally trained in classical and quantum chaos. His research interests are focused on open quantum systems – electron transport, quantum computing – and magnetic properties of nanostructures.

Amanda Chatten is a lecturer leading research on the luminescent solar concentrator in the Department of Physics at Imperial College London. Her work focuses on developing theoretical models and characterisation techniques for the concentrator with the aim of increasing device efficiency by exploiting the potential of nanomaterials and improving light management.

David Clements is a lecturer in Astrophysics at Imperial College London working on extragalactic astronomy and observational cosmology. He is involved with the ESA Herschel and Planck satellites and has used data from previous generations of infrared space observatories as well Hubble, Chandra and numerous ground-based telescopes. He also has an interest in science fiction and has recently had a number of short stories published.

Peter Coles is Professor of Theoretical Astrophysics at Cardiff University. His primary research interest is in cosmology and the large-scale structure of the universe. He works on theoretical aspects of this problem, with an emphasis on statistical techniques to test models of structure formation against observations. He is also interested in exotic cosmological models and in analytic techniques for studying the growth of large-scale structure in the expanding universe.

Shin Egashira worked in Tokyo, Beijing and New York before coming to London, and has exhibited artwork and architectural installations worldwide. He is the author of Before Object, After Image (AA Publications, 2006), which documented a decade-long summer workshop he has organised in the remote village of Koshirakura. He has been running his own Diploma Unit at the AA for over ten years.

Alberto Garutti has become a prominent advocate of community-sensitive, anti-monumental public art over the last decade. He is a teacher at Milan's Accademia di Brera and IUAV Venice. His projects have included a modest cubic pavilion on the periphery of Bolzano and an outdoor light installation on a bridge spanning the Bosphorus that registered each birth at a nearby maternity hospital.

Andrew Jaffe is a cosmologist. He works on various topics including the formation of structure in the universe and gravitational radiation, but most of his research involves the Cosmic Microwave Background (CMB). He has been involved in the analysis of data from various experiments observing the CMB, starting with the MAXIMA and BOOMERaNG balloons which were the first to use maps of the CMB to measure the curvature of the universe.

Peter Liversidge has worked in many mediums, including drawing, painting, sculpture, installation and performance. A key aspect of his practice and preparation for exhibitions is the submission of typed and posted proposals, which may or may not be acted on.

Julian Loeffler studied architecture in Austria and at the AA where he graduated with honours in 2004. He has worked for Herzog & de Meuron in Basel and taught at the AA with Pascal Schöning. He is currently based in London where he is involved in a number of architectural and multidisciplinary projects, while doing research into cinematic architecture.

John Palmesino and **Ann-Sofi Rönnskog** are founders of Territorial Agency, an independent organisation that combines architectural analysis, projects, advocacy and action for the integrated spatial transformation of contemporary territories. Ann-Sofi previously was a researcher and studied in Helsinki, Copenhagen and Zurich. John is currently pursuing a PhD at Goldsmiths, and was the head of a research group on international cities at ETH Zurich and Studio Basel/Contemporary City Institute with Jacques Herzog and Pierre de Meuron. He is the co-founder of multiplicity in Milan.

Wilfredo Prieto was born in Cuba. He has a university diploma as a painter but he hasn't painted anything for the last ten years. He admires conceptual art but tries to distance himself from any traditional way of making art and also tries to stay free of any particular historical or cultural considerations that could hinder his creativity. He works in a variety of media, depending on the nature of each particular piece of work.

Stefano Rabolli Pansera graduated with honours from the AA. He has worked for Herzog & de Meuron and is currently teaching at the AA. He has lectured in Naples and at Cambridge University, has been visiting professor at Cagliari and has taught in several of the AA Visiting Schools. He is founder of Rabolli Pansera Ltd.

Riccardo Rossi is a freelance engineer working for private and public companies as well as several research institutes. Most of his work is concerned with energy and industrial processes, including power plants, vehicle power and design, transportation and mobility. For a number of years he has collaborated with artists and galleries on specific projects, providing engineering designs and assistance.

Salottobuono was founded in 2005 as a collective of research and design production. It investigates urban space, codifying cognitive devices and triggering transformation strategies. Topics, challenges and programmes are occasions for diagrammatic analyses and elaborations of paradoxical visions. Critical nodes, discontinuities and weak points are exasperated through the formulation of visionary objects and performative practices.

Ariel Schlesinger was born in Jerusalem and moved to Santa Cruz, CA, before leaving school. Since then his inspiration has been drawn from other individuals, locations, cities and activities. In his artistic practice he reverses the order of production, going back from the finished item to the prototype, restoring its identity and inventing it anew.

Vid Stojevic completed his MSc in Quantum Fields and Fundamental Forces, an MSci in Physics at Imperial College and a PhD in Theoretical Physics at King's College London. He then moved forward to a postdoc at the Institute of Theoretical Physics at the University of Hamburg. His scientific interests include string theory.

Roberto Trotta is a cosmologist in the Astrophysics Group of Imperial College London where he is a lecturer in Physics. He takes part in numerous public engagements with scientific activities, from science festivals to radio broadcasts. From 2005 to 2008 he was the Lockyer Research Fellow of the Royal Astronomical Society at the Astrophysics Department of Oxford University and has been a Junior Fellow of St Anne's College.

Eyal Weizman is an architect and director of the Centre for Research Architecture at Goldsmiths, University of London. He studied architecture at the AA and completed his PhD at the London Consortium/Birkbeck College. He is a member of the architectural collective 'decolonising architecture' in Beit Sahour/Palestine. Weizman is a regular contributor and editorial board member for Humanity, Cabinet and Inflexions.

Ines Weizman trained as an architect at the Bauhaus University Weimar and the École d'Architecture de Belleville in Paris, later studying at Cambridge University and the AA. She completed her PhD in History and Theory of Architecture in 2004 at the AA. In her research she studies the effects of the collapse of the Iron Curtain on the urbanism of former Soviet countries and recently also works on authenticity, originality and copyright in architecture. She currently teaches at London Metropolitan University and the AA.

Participants in the Beyond Entropy Symposium at Fondazione Giorgio Cini, Venice included:

Brett Steele	Ricky Burdett
Hans Ulrich Obrist	Marco Baravalle
Bonnie Camplin	Harald Thys
Matteo Pasquinelli	Alessio Satta
Grazia Francescato	Arazzi Laptop Ensemble
Nikolaus Hirsch	Reinier De Graaf
Angelo Merlino	Nur Puri Purini
Fabio Eboli	Antonio Negri
Tania Saxl	Judith Revel
Joel Newman	Giuseppe Caccia
Javier Castañon	Francesco Garutti
Joseph Rykwert	Aaron Levy
Alessandro Marini	Christian von Düring
Marco Vanucci	Charles Jencks
Stefano Boeri	Shumon Basar

ACKNOWLEDGEMENTS

Special thanks go to the sponsors of Beyond Entropy:
Olivetti – Direct Technology Solutions; Bersi Serlini; RePower;
and the media partner Abitare.

We would also like to thank Manuela Luca' Dazio and Paolo
Scibelli at the Fondazione La Biennale di Venezia and Pasquale
Gagliardi and Maria Novella Benzoni at the Fondazione Giorgio
Cini Onlus.

At the Architectural Association warm thanks go to Brett Steele,
Charles Tashima, Stephen Livett, Esther McLaughlin, Vanessa
Norwood, Frank Owen, Rosa Ainley, Zak Kyes, Valerie Bennett,
Wayne Daly, Lee Regan, Luke Currall, Thomas Weaver, Pamela
Johnston and Mark Campbell.

Additional thanks to Jan Nauta, Aram Mooradian, Silvana
Taher, Merlin Eayrs, Conrad Koslowsky, Scrap Marshall,
Artemis Doupa and Jack Self.

SHUMON BASAR

THE END

'It's the end of the night', he says.
'It's the end of the world', she says.

His BlackBerry buzzes.

The battery is nearly kaput. He's had it on for half an hour a day.

A power cut grips Giudecca.

Tomorrow will be a month. 'I can see the stars for the first time', he says.

She replies, 'I miss the anxious flicker of fluorescent lights. I miss ice cubes and frozen pizza. I miss electricity.'

They exasperate, 'Why are we the generation who lived to see the end of oil? Coal? Gas?'

They fail to get the paradox: if
all matter is potential energy,
how can energy ever run out?

More wars will be fought,
more energy expended, more
matter destroyed to ensure that
our energy never ends.

'It's the end of the world', she says.

He has only one response,
'No. It's the end of the night'.

COLOPHON

Beyond Entropy
Edited by Stefano Rabolli Pansera

Book Editor: Mark Campbell
Design: Z.A.K.
Transcriptions: Marlie Mul

Printed in Germany by GGP Media GmbH, Pössneck

ISBN 978-1-907896-06-4

For a catalogue of AA Publications visit
aaschool.ac.uk/publications
or email publications@aaschool.ac.uk

AA Publications
36 Bedford Square
London WC1B 3ES
T + 44(0)20 7887 4021
F + 44(0)20 7414 0783